CAMBRIDGE STUDIES  S0-AWT-588

What is a Law of Nature?

CAMBRIDGE STUDIES IN PHILOSOPHY

General editor SYDNEY SHOEMAKER

Advisory editors J. E. J. ALTHAM, SIMON BLACKBURN,
GILBERT HARMAN, MARTIN HOLLIS, FRANK JACKSON,
JONATHAN LEAR, JOHN PERRY, T. J. SMILEY, BARRY STROUD

What is a Law of Nature?

D. M. Armstrong

Challis Professor of Philosophy
University of Sydney

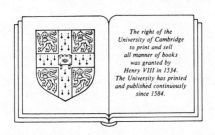

The right of the
University of Cambridge
to print and sell
all manner of books
was granted by
Henry VIII in 1534.
The University has printed
and published continuously
since 1584.

Cambridge University Press

Cambridge
London   New York   New Rochelle
Melbourne   Sydney

Published by the Press Syndicate of the University of Cambridge
The Pitt Building. Trumpington Street, Cambridge CB2 1RP
32 East 57th Street, New York. NY 10022, USA
10 Stamford Road, Oakleigh, Melbourne 3166, Australia

First published 1983
First paperback edition 1985
Reprinted 1987

Printed in Great Britain by
Redwood Burn Limited
Trowbridge, Wiltshire

Library of Congress catalogue card number 83–5130

British Library Cataloguing in Publication Data
Armstrong, D. M.
What is a law of nature?—
(Cambridge Studies in Philosophy)
1. Natural law
I. Title   II. Series
171'.2   K460

ISBN 0521 25343 8 hard covers
ISBN 0 521 31481 X paperback

RB–

For Jenny

Contents

Acknowledgements

I am conscious of great debts to many people in the composition of this work. I would like to thank John Bacon, Michael Bradley, Gregory Currie, Peter Forrest, Laurence Goldstein, Herbert Hochberg, Frank Jackson, Bruce Langtry, David Lewis, Chris Mortensen, Len O'Neill, David Sanford, Jack Smart, David Stove, Richard Swinburne, Chris Swoyer, Martin Tweedale, Peter Van Inwagen and John Watkins. I hope that I have not left anybody out. Specific acknowledgements on particular points are made in the text. But I have received so much valuable comment that I know that there is some of it which I have failed to assimilate and profit from. I have also learnt a great deal from my students in the course of giving seminars on the Laws of Nature at the University of Sydney and the University of Texas at Austin. I should like to thank Anthea Bankoff, Pat Trifonoff and Jackie Walter for much typing and retyping of drafts.

I leave to the last mention of my quite special debt to Michael Tooley. As I hope that the text makes clear, he has everywhere influenced my thinking on this thorny and difficult topic of the nature of the laws of nature.

Sydney University   D. M. A.
1982

PART I

A critique of
the Regularity theory

1

Introductory

1 THE IMPORTANCE OF OUR TOPIC

The question 'What is a law of nature?' is a central question for the philosophy of science. But its importance goes beyond this relatively restricted context to embrace general epistemology and metaphysics. In this section I will first discuss the importance of the question for the philosophy of science and then its importance in the wider context.

Natural science traditionally concerns itself with at least three tasks. The first is to discover the geography and history of the universe, taking 'geography' to cover all space and 'history' to cover all time, including future time. Astronomy is beginning to give us a picture of how the universe as a whole is laid out in space and time. Some other natural sciences give us an overview of more restricted spatio-temporal areas.

A second task is to discover what sorts of thing and what sorts of property there are in the universe and how they are constituted, with particular emphasis upon the sorts of thing and the sorts of property in terms of which other things are explained. (These explainers may or may not be ultimate explainers.)

The third task is to state the laws which the things in space and time obey. Or, putting it in the terms used in describing the second task, the third task is to state the laws which link sort of thing with sort of thing, and property with property.

It may not be obvious that there is a second task to be distinguished from the third. But consider the scientific discovery that heat is molecular motion. It is obvious that this is not a historical/geographical truth. I shall argue at a later point that it is not a law of nature, even a 'bridge law' (Ch. 10, Sec. 1). It is something different: it gives the constitution of a property, or range of properties, in terms of more ultimate properties. (It could be said to give the 'geography' of a property.)

3

What is true is that the three enquiries are inextricably bound up with each other. They logically presuppose each other and can only be pursued in conjunction with each other. Nevertheless, they are distinguishable.

If the discovery of the laws of nature is one of the three great traditional tasks of natural science, then the nature of a law of nature must be a central ontological concern for the philosophy of science. As for the importance of science itself, I take its 'vanguard role' in the gaining of knowledge and/or reasonable belief about the world to be obvious enough.

However, our question 'What is a law of nature?' is of still wider philosophical importance. To see why, we may appeal to Hume. Hume said (*Treatise*, Bk 1, Pt III, Sec. II) that the *only* relation which enables us to infer from observed matters of fact to unobserved matters of fact is the relation of cause and effect. If no such relation existed, we would have no way to reason beyond our observations.

Hume spoke little of laws. Nevertheless, it can be said that he held a law theory of cause and effect. Setting aside the mental component which he found in our concept of cause, he conceived of the relation between cause and effect as a law-like relation. (The law in turn he conceived of as a mere regularity.) We can therefore invoke his authority to say that inferences to particular matters of unobserved fact would not be reliable inferences if there were no laws of nature.

But it is hardly required that we appeal to Hume. The proposition is obvious enough in itself. The scientist trying to establish the geography and history of the unobserved portion of the universe must depend upon what he takes to be the laws of the universe. Otherwise he is helpless. (It is true also, of course, that what he takes the laws to be will in part depend upon what he takes the history and geography to be.) In ordinary life, by contrast, when making inferences to particular matters of unobserved fact, we make little appeal to, and would be unable to state, the supposed laws which ground our inferences. But it is still the case that, on the supposition that there are no laws, the inferences would not be rational.

As Hume understood and emphasized, inference from the observed to the unobserved is central to our whole life as human beings. We have just seen, however, that if there were no laws (whatever a law is, be it regularity or something else), then such inferences would not be reliable. Hence the notion of law is, or should be, a central concept for epistemology. If so, we will also want to enquire into its ontology. We will want to know what a law of nature *is*.

There is one truly eccentric view, brought to my attention by Peter Forrest, which would evade this argument. This is the view that, although there are regularities in the world, there are no laws of nature. Such a view agrees with critics of the Regularity theory of law that mere regularities are insufficient for law. But, in Eliminativist spirit, it goes on to deny that the world contains anything except these regularities. This Disappearance view of law can nevertheless maintain that inferences to the unobserved are reliable, because, although the world is not law-governed, it is, by luck or for some other reason, regular.

Such a view, however, will have to face the question what good reason we can have to think that the world is regular. It will have to face the Problem of Induction. It will be argued in Chapter 4, Section 5, that no Regularity theorist, whether or not he is prepared to call his regularities 'laws', can escape inductive scepticism.

2 A POSSIBLE DIFFICULTY IN INVESTIGATING OUR TOPIC

So much by way of apologia for our topic. But it may seem to be somewhat recalcitrant to philosophical investigation. Here we may recall Socrates' and G. E. Moore's 'Paradox of Analysis'. If we ask what sort of thing an X is (a right act, a law of nature . . .) then either we know what an X is, or we do not. If we know, then there is no need to ask the question. If we do not know, then there is no way to begin the investigation. The enquiry is either pointless or impossible.

The orthodox, and I think correct, solution of this puzzle is that we do not start with blank ignorance of what an X is. Instead, we start with an unreflective, unselfconscious or merely practical grasp of the thing. The philosophical object is to pass from this to an articulate, explicit and reasoned grasp of what an X is. We do not go from black night to daylight, but from twilight to daylight.

In such investigations it is a great advantage, to say the least, if we can securely identify instances of X. Given such *paradigms*, we can to some extent tie the enquiry down. An account of what it is to be an X is suggested by a philosopher. If we can be sure that *a* is an X, then we can use other things which we know or believe about *a* to check

5

the proposed account of X. But without paradigms the whole business of testing the proposal becomes very much more difficult.

Our problem is now before us. There are no secure paradigms of laws of nature. Consider contemporary natural science. It is perfectly possible, epistemically possible, that we do not know a single law of nature. This, it may be objected, is a considerable handicap to answering the philosophical question 'What is a law of nature?'

To this objection, two answers may be made.

First, even though we can point to no secure paradigms of laws, the scientific theories which we now work with are obviously a reasonable approximation to at least some of the real laws of nature. For if our theories did not nearly grasp the truth at many points, it would be inexplicable that they should permit so much successful prediction. Theoretical calculations which can return men from the moon with split-second accuracy can hardly be mere fantasies. We may make an 'inference to the best explanation' from the predictive success of contemporary scientific theory to the conclusion that such theory mirrors at least some of the laws of nature over some part of their range with tolerable accuracy.

Actually, it seems that even the rough-and-ready generalizations of pre-scientific practical wisdom represent a reasonable degree of approximation to genuine laws. Consider Hume's examples: fire burns, bread nourishes, water suffocates. If there were not laws to which these generalizations represent some rough approximation, then we should all be dead.

It may be remarked in passing that this first reply to the objection from the absence of paradigms indicates the importance, in the fight against scepticism, of developing a satisfactory theory of degrees of closeness to the truth, a theory of partial truth.

The second answer to the objection is that, even if we know no laws, we do know the *forms* which statements of law take. Consider the following formulae which use dummies:

(1) It is a law that Fs are Gs
(2) It is a law that an F has a certain probability (> 0, < 1) of being a G
(3) It is a law that the quantities P and Q co-vary in such a way that Q is a certain function of P ($Q = f(P)$).

It turns out, as a matter of fact, that the sort of fundamental investigation which we are undertaking can largely proceed with mere schemata of this sort. After all, it is not as if philosophers can expect to make any serious contribution to the *scientific* project of establishing what in fact the laws of nature are! Our abstract formulae may actually exhibit the heart of many philosophical problems about laws of nature, disentangled from confusing empirical detail. To every subject, its appropriate level of abstraction.

If more concrete examples are required, then we can take them from current or earlier science. We now know that Newton's Law of Universal Gravitation is not really a law. Yet we also know that Newton's formula approximates to the truth for at least a wide range of phenomena. Its predictive power would be inexplicable otherwise. So it makes a very good stand-in for a paradigm of a law of nature.

In this essay the abstract formula considered will often be (1): It is a law that Fs are Gs. In fact, arguing from the present state of science, it does not seem very likely that many laws are of this form. It would appear, for instance, that the laws governing sub-atomic phenomena are both irreducibly probabilistic and are functional. They have a form which combines (2) and (3).[1] But the peculiar simplicity of (1) makes it extremely useful for discussing a number of difficult philosophical issues concerning laws. These issues would emerge less clearly in more complex contexts.

3 ASSUMPTIONS

Some of the presuppositions of this enquiry have already emerged. In this section I will mention three further assumptions that I will make. I hope that they will not remain assumptions merely, but that some considerations in their favour will emerge in the course of the discussion. But since they are rather fundamental, and so not easily argued for, and since they are also somewhat controversial, it seems desirable to put them explicitly before the reader.

First, I assume the truth of a Realistic account of laws of nature. That is to say, I assume that they exist independently of the minds which attempt to grasp them. (Just what sort of thing they are, it is the task of this essay to investigate. It is clear, simply from considering the typical forms of law-statements, that a law is some sort of

---

[1] It may be argued that both (2) and (3) can be reduced to form (1). My reasons for rejecting both these reductions will emerge. See Ch. 3, Sec. 4 for (2) and Ch. 7 for (3).

complex entity.) Laws of nature must therefore be sharply distinguished from law-*statements*. Law-statements may be true or (much more likely) false. If they are true, then what makes them true is a law.

The task of the critic of anti-Realist views of laws has been greatly eased by the recent publication of a fine and scholarly article by Alan Musgrave (1981). What he offers is primarily a critique of Wittgensteinian Instrumentalism about laws, as it is found in the *Tractatus*, and in Wittgenstein's followers W. H. Watson, Toulmin, Hanson and Harré. But there is also useful criticism of other anti-Realist positions.

In any case, however, behind all anti-Realist views of laws stands the Regularity theory. After all, those who do not take a Realistic view of laws have to allow that there is *some* foundation in the world for the acceptability or otherwise of law-statements. At this point they must appeal to regularities. Regularities are the Realistic component of anti-Realist theories of laws. As a result, a destructive critique of the Regularity theory, the business of the first Part of this essay, will simultaneously undermine anti-Realist theories of laws.

Second, to this Realism about laws, I add a more specific Realism: Realism about universals. As a matter of fact, I do not think that even the Regularity view can be coherently developed, at least in a Realistic way, without the introduction of universals (Ch. 2, Sec. 4). But, as we shall see (Ch. 6, Sec. 1), the Realist about laws who wishes to go beyond the Regularity theory must certainly invoke universals.

Theories of universals are developed in different ways, and these differences place different constraints upon theories of laws of nature which involve universals. My own Realism about universals is developed in a previous book, *Universals and Scientific Realism* (1978). No acquaintance with that work is presupposed, but in this essay I will state my views about universals (Ch. 6, Sec. 2), and take these views are constraints on my theory of laws. *Arguments* for these views are to be found only in the earlier work. To that extent, this monograph is a sequel to the book on universals. That book's last chapter put forward what now seems to me to be a somewhat primitive form of the view of laws of nature defended in the present work.

Third, in this essay I assume the truth of what may be called Actualism. According to this view, we should not postulate any

8

particulars except actual particulars, nor any properties and re-lations (universals) save actual, or categorical, properties and relations. I do not think that this should debar us from thinking that both the past and the future exist, or are real. But it does debar us from admitting into our ontology the merely possible, not only the merely logically possible but also the merely physically possible.

This debars us from postulating such properties as dispositions and powers where these are conceived of as properties over and above the categorical properties of objects. It is not denied that state-ments attributing dispositions and/or powers to objects, or sorts of objects, are often true. But the truth-makers or ontological ground for such true statements must always be found in the actual, or cat-egorical, properties of the objects involved.

I regard Actualism as the most difficult and uncertain of my three assumptions. It is bound up with the difficult question whether the laws of nature involve logical necessities in things: whether there is *de re* logical necessity involved in laws. For dispositions and powers, if they are conceived of as the non-Actualist conceives them, involve logical or quasi-logical connections in the world between the dispositions and powers, on the one hand, and their actualizations on the other.

4 THE REGULARITY THEORY

It is convenient to begin by examining and criticizing the Regularity analysis of laws of nature. The credit of this theory does not stand as high as it used to. But, although somewhat battered, it is still ortho-doxy among analytic philosophers. In particular, there are still many who would *like* it to be true. While this liking persists, we can expect it to have a powerful, if not always acknowledged, influence. So it is still important to work through the theory in detail, and see just how unsatisfactory it is.

Nor will the value of a discussion of the Regularity theory be critical and therapeutic only. In the course of the criticisms a number of considerations will be introduced which will lead us toward a more satisfactory account of laws of nature, if only by showing us what a good theory of laws ought to do.

With the Regularity theory disposed of, it will then be argued that

9

any satisfactory account of laws of nature must involve universals, and irreducible relations between them. This opens up a new, by no means easy, but exciting programme of philosophical research. The second part of this essay attempts to advance the programme.

2

Critique of the Regularity theory (1): The problem of accidental uniformities

Laws of nature characteristically *manifest* themselves or *issue* in regularities. It is natural, therefore, in Ockhamist spirit, to consider whether laws are anything more than these manifestations.

When philosophers hear the phrase 'Regularity theory' they are inclined almost automatically to think of a Regularity theory of *causation*. It is important, therefore, to be clear at the outset that what is being considered here is a Regularity theory of *laws*.

The Regularity theory of causation appears to be a conjunction of two propositions: (1) that causal connection is a species of law-like connection; (2) that laws are nothing but regularities in the behaviour of things. It is possible to deny the truth of (1), as Singularist theories of causation do, and then go on either to assert or to deny the truth of (2). Alternatively, (1) can be upheld, and either (2) asserted (yielding the Regularity theory of causation), or (2) denied. The reduction of cause to law, and the reduction of law to regularity, are two independent doctrines. They can be accepted or rejected independently.

It therefore appears that the Regularity theory of causation entails the Regularity theory of laws of nature, because the latter theory is a proper part of the former. By the same token, the Regularity theory of laws of nature fails to entail the Regularity theory of causation. Our concern is with the Regularity theory of law.

1 THE NAIVE REGULARITY THEORY OF LAW

There are different versions of the Regularity theory. Effective criticisms of one version may fail to be effective criticisms of another, leading to a certain amount of confusion. George Molnar (1969) provides us with a good strategy in this situation. He begins by outlining a theory which he calls the Regularity theory of laws of

11

nature, but which I shall call the *Naive Regularity* theory. He then considers an important argument against such a theory advanced by William Kneale, an argument from unrealized physical possibilities. Molnar claims that Kneale's argument succeeds against the theory which he, Molnar, has outlined. However, numerous modifications of this theory can be proposed, with the object of meeting Kneale's and other criticisms. Molnar therefore goes on to consider whether the theory can be rescued from Kneale's attack by means of judicious modifications which still respect the spirit of the theory. He argues, however, that when these proposed modifications are scrutinized, none are found to be satisfactory. He concludes that there is no acceptable form of the Regularity theory. It cannot be modified, it must be abandoned.

I propose to generalize Molnar's strategy. I agree with his estimation of the force of Kneale's argument. But I think that there are many other arguments which either refute, or tell heavily against, the Regularity theory. It is very convenient to advance these as arguments against the Naive theory in the first place, and only after that to consider whether they can be evaded by more sophisticated versions of the theory.

Molnar defines the Naive Regularity theory by using the device of semantic ascent. He says:

p is a *statement* of a law of nature if and only if:
   (i)   *p* is universally quantified
   (ii)   *p* is [omnitemporally and omnispatially][1] true
   (iii) *p* is contingent
   (iv)   *p* contains only non-local empirical predicates, apart from logical connectives and quantifiers.

There is much in this definition which could be discussed, but which I pass over for the present. I think it will serve our current purposes. It is easy to see the aim of the definition: to pick out the *unrestricted* or *cosmic* uniformities from all other uniformities in nature. I will call them *Humean* uniformities, for obvious reasons. These Humean uniformities the Naive Regularity theory identifies with the laws of nature.

2 CLASSIFICATION OF CRITICISMS OF THE REGULARITY THEORY

If we take the Humean uniformities and try to identify them with the laws of nature, then various difficulties for the identification

[1] David Lewis has pointed out to me that the bracketed phrase is redundant.

arise. First, there are what may be broadly termed extensional difficulties. There are, or there appear to be, Humean uniformities which are not laws of nature. That is, being a Humean uniformity is not sufficient for being a law of nature. Again there are, or at least there could be, laws which do not hold over all space and time. There are also probabilistic laws. Neither of these sorts of law involve Humean uniformities.[2] That is, being a Humean uniformity is not necessary for a law of nature. The failure of sufficiency will be the subject of this chapter, the failure of necessity the subject in the earlier sections of the next chapter.

Even if all these difficulties can be overcome, and I do not believe that they can be, plenty of difficulties remain for the Regularity theory of laws. That theory envisages a very simple relationship between a law and its associated Humean uniformity. It is a law that Fs are Gs if and only if all Fs are Gs, where the latter is a Humean uniformity. The content of the law and the content of the uniformity are identical. However, there appear to be cases where a law and its manifestation are not related in this straightforward way. A gap can open up between law and manifestation of law. Two sorts of case will be discussed in the last two sections of the next chapter, involving probabilistic and functional laws.

Finally, there are what might be called 'intensional' difficulties. Suppose that there is a Humean uniformity to which a law does correspond, and suppose that the content of the uniformity is the same as the content of the law. Even so, there are a number of reasons for thinking that the law and the uniformity are not identical. For the law has properties which the manifestation lacks. These difficulties will be discussed in Chapter 4.

In Chapter 5 we will consider attempts to meet some of these difficulties by sophisticating the Naive Regularity theory. The failure of these sophisticating attempts should leave us intellectually and psychologically well prepared to look for a replacement for the Regularity theory.

3 SINGLE-CASE UNIFORMITIES

It has long been recognized, even by Regularity theorists themselves, that the laws of nature are, at best, a mere sub-class of the

---

[2] Although we shall see that there is a strategy which attempts to reinterpret probabilistic laws as a special sort of uniformity.

class of Humean uniformities. A recognized research programme for contemporary Regularity theorists is to find a way to cut out unwanted Humean uniformities while still remaining faithful to the spirit of the Regularity theory. For the present, however, we are concerned to make a case against the *Naive* Regularity theory, which simply identifies laws and Humean uniformities. Various objections show that this identification is indeed naive. I begin by considering single-case uniformities. It is clear that they are ubiquitous. Yet in general they are not associated with laws of nature.

It is probable that every object in the universe differs in its properties from everything else. I mean here by 'properties' *general*, that is, non-local, properties. On this understanding, *living in Australia* is not a property. In the case of microscopic objects, such as electrons, it may be necessary to include relational properties in order to ensure that the objects differ from each other in properties. The relational properties must again be non-local. *Being a light-second distant from proton A* is not a general relational property, but *being a light-second distant from a proton* would be satisfactory. In the case of macroscopic objects, however, it is not even necessary to appeal to relational properties. Consider, for instance, the exact shape, size and arrangement of the microscopic constituents of two identical-seeming ball-bearings. These properties of shape, size and arrangement of constituents have the advantage that, even on quite restrictive theories of properties, they will count as genuine properties. They may, of course, be idiosyncratic and uninteresting properties. But they will serve to differentiate all macroscopic objects.

For each particular, therefore, it is likely that there exists at least one *individuating conjunction* of properties, that is, a conjunction of properties such that the particular instantiates this conjunction and nothing else does. The vast majority, at least, of these individuating conjunctions will be non-exhaustive, that is, will fail to exhaust the nature of the particular in question. The particular will have further properties. Where there is an individuating conjunction which thus fails to exhaust the nature of a particular, call the set of the further properties of that particular the 'remainder set'.

The existence of an indefinitely numerous set of Humean uniformities now becomes obvious. Its members are constituted by antecedents involving (non-exhaustive) individuating conjunctions of properties. The consequents will involve a property drawn from

14

the corresponding remainder sets. It is true that, in the case of all these uniformities, there can never be any more than one instance associated with each uniformity. But they will be Humean uniformities nevertheless.

In general, however, we do not think that these uniformities are laws of nature.

It may be thought that single-case uniformities are somewhat degenerate cases of Humean uniformities. It is therefore important to realize that a Regularity theorist cannot deal with the problem which they raise simply by not counting them as Humean uniformities. For although, in general, single-case uniformities are not manifestations of laws of nature, it is perfectly thinkable, and may be the case, that some are. Some individuating conjunctions of properties may be such that it is a law that if and only if a particular instantiates that conjunction then the particular will have a certain further property.

In causal contexts, indeed, single-case uniformities which are manifestations of a corresponding law might easily occur. Suppose that certain complex and idiosyncratic conditions give rise to idiosyncratic emergent effects, and suppose that this causal sequence is law-governed. It is easy to imagine that these conditions occur only once. We will have a single-case Humean uniformity which is a manifestation of a corresponding law.

4 HOW TO PASS FROM SINGLE-CASE UNIFORMITIES TO MULTI-CASE UNIFORMITIES

In any case, as David Blumenfeld has pointed out to me, given a plurality of single-case Humean uniformities, we can immediately construct plural-case Humean uniformities which, however, we have no reason to believe are manifestations of laws of nature. All we do is to point to uniformities of the following sort. Consider individuating conjunctions of properties A, B and C, associated with distinct particulars, a, b and c. We can then say that whenever an object is of the sort (A or B or C), then it further has the property (A$\star$ or B$\star$ or C$\star$). The latter disjuncts are properties drawn from the remainder sets associated with A, B and C respectively.

But why is this disjunctive state of affairs to be accounted a *uniformity*? The problem, of course, is how to exclude it. Disjunctive

15

predicates must be used in setting up the case. But what objection is there to saying that these disjunctive predicates pick out properties? Suppose that a single predicate 'M' is introduced in place of 'A or B or C', and 'N' instead of 'A★ or B★ or C★'. Each M is an N. Why is this not a Humean uniformity having just three instances? Certainly, it would be permitted by Molnar's definition of a uniformity (Sec. 1). Molnar says (on behalf of Regularity theorists) that 'p', the statement of the law of nature, must contain only non-local empirical predicates. The schematic predicates just introduced respect that condition. Yet surely Blumenfeld's uniformities are mere pseudo-uniformities?

The problem is a close relative of the problem introduced by Nelson Goodman (1954) with his famous predicates 'grue' and 'bleen'.[3] Suppose that all green things were to turn blue after 2000 A.D., and all blue things green. Relative to the predicates 'green' and 'blue' the things change. But it would be possible to introduce a pair of predicates 'grue' and 'bleen' relative to which the things did not change. A green thing which became blue at that date would be said to be still grue, while a blue thing which became green would be accounted still bleen. Relative to these new predicates, a green thing which remained green through 2000 A.D. or a blue thing which remained blue, *changed* at that time. The problem is to say why one set of predicates should have preference over the other.

Returning to our own problem, it is clear that if the Regularity account of laws of nature is to be developed in a Realistic way it must be stipulated that only *certain* non-local predicates can be used to state 'uniformities'. Admissable predicates must carve reality along some joint, must pick out a natural, or unified, or objectively resembling, class of phenomena. Otherwise the 'uniformities' are not *uniformities*.

Historically, defenders of Regularity theories have tended to be Nominalists, that is, deniers of universals. But Blumenfeld's difficulty seems to show that a Realistic version, at least, of a Regularity theory of laws will have to postulate universals. How else will it be possible to say that the different instances of a certain uniformity are all instances of objectively the *same* phenomenon? (Another possibility is to try to construct resemblance-classes based upon objective

---

[3] As is often done in contemporary discussion, I will not use Goodman's own definitions. Instead I will adopt simpler definitions which are more convenient for my purposes.

resemblances which, however, are not grounded upon common properties. But I do not believe that such a 'Resemblance Nominalism' is a satisfactory account. See my 1978, Ch. 5.)

5 HOW TO PASS FROM LOCAL UNIFORMITIES TO HUMEAN UNIFORMITIES

The single-case argument shows how likely it is that there are indefinite numbers of Humean uniformities which are not laws of nature. This is a grave embarrassment to any Regularity theory. Ayer (1956) has pointed out that by starting with *local* uniformities, it is easy to see that, associated with each of them, there are Humean uniformities which, in general, are not laws of nature. These new Humean uniformities will be plural-case manifestations.

Consider any plural-case local uniformity, for instance that everybody in a certain room is wearing a wrist-watch. It is overwhelmingly likely that there is a Humean uniformity associated with this local uniformity. It is necessary only that there be an individuating conjunction of (non-local) properties associated with the room. The people in the room will then be all and only those objects which (a) are people, (b) have the relational property of *being within* an object having that set of individuating properties. It will be a Humean uniformity that people having these properties all wear wrist-watches. But such uniformities will not in general be (or be manifestations of) laws of nature. At the same time, it cannot be logically excluded that some of these uniformities are in fact laws of nature.

6 UNREALIZED PHYSICAL POSSIBILITIES

We now turn to consider Kneale's argument against the Naive Regularity theory, the argument from unrealized physical (empirical, nomic) possibilities (1950, 1961).

We ordinarily assume, in a relatively pre-theoretical way, that there are physical possibilities which are omnitemporally never realized. We believe that there never was nor will be a solid lump of gold with a volume greater than a cubic mile. Yet we also believe that such a piece of gold cannot be logically ruled out simply on the basis of the laws of nature. Such a piece of gold is an unrealized physical possibility. It may be contrasted with a lump of uranium-

17

235 with a volume greater than a cubic mile. If we temporarily prescind from the possibility that the laws involved are merely probabilistic, then the lump of uranium is a physical impossibility, because 'critical mass' would be exceeded.

What Kneale points out is that, given the Naive Regularity theory of law, there cannot be any unrealized physical possibilities.

The following case given by Kneale (1950) illustrates the argument. Consider the possibility that a whole race of ravens (as opposed to mere sports) should have white plumage. This has never been the case, and, we may assume, will never be the case. However, evolutionary theory gives us good reason to think that, if a race of ravens came to inhabit permanently snowy regions, that race would eventually be a white-feathered race. A race of white ravens is therefore an unrealized physical possibility. But it is a Humean uniformity that no race of ravens is white-feathered. Hence, if the Naive Regularity analysis of law is correct, it is a law that no race of ravens is white-feathered, that is, such a race is physically impossible. A most unwelcome result of the theory.

Karl Popper (1959, pp. 427–8) has contributed an imaginary case concerning moas, flightless New Zealand birds which have been extinct for some centuries. He supposes that every moa died before the age of fifty years. This appears to create a Humean uniformity. The number of moas throughout all time is presumably finite, but it is potentially infinite. Popper now further supposes that there is nothing in the genetic constitution of moas which prevents them living beyond fifty years. Rather, it was the presence of a certain virus in the New Zealand environment which caused each moa to die before it was fifty. In an otherwise similar, but virus-free, environment, some moas would have lived beyond fifty years.

Popper thus gave a sketch of an unrealized physical possibility. But, given the Naive Regularity view of laws, it is a law that moas die before fifty, for this is a Humean uniformity. Hence it is physically impossible that a moa should live beyond fifty.

The same argument can be mounted in the case of any *general* unrealized physical possibility. Given the Naive Regularity view of laws, it will be a law that such possibilities are unrealized. They will be logically possible, but not physically possible.

It should be noted that it is possible to assimilate the argument from single-case Humean uniformities (Sec. 3), and from Humean uniformities generated from local uniformities (Sec. 5), to this objection from unrealized physical possibilities. For, in both sorts of case, the reason for thinking that these uniformities are unlikely to be manifestations of laws is that it seems physically possible that the antecedent properties of these uniformities should have been instantiated, yet the consequent properties not have been instantiated. Perhaps the importance of these two arguments is that they show how easy it is to point to vast multitudes of unrealized physical possibilities, each of which raises a problem for the Naive Regularity theory of laws.

7 HUMEAN UNIFORMITIES WITH NON-EXISTENT SUBJECTS

Contemporary logic renders a Humean uniformity by expressions of the form '$(x) (Fx \supset Gx)$', or some more complex expression of a material implication preceded by a universal quantifier. It is notorious that such a formula expresses a true proposition if there are no Fs. For the statement is a statement about everything, saying of each thing that *either* that thing is not an F, *or* if it is an F, then it is a G. Hence, given that everything is not an F, the statement is true. Given further that 'F' and 'G' are suitable predicates, then '$(x) (Fx \supset Gx)$' is a statement of a Humean uniformity.

It apparently follows that, on the Naive Regularity view of laws of nature, it is a law of nature that centaurs are peculiarly adept at philosophy, simply because, omnitemporally, there are no centaurs. It is also a law of nature that centaurs are quite unable to take in the simplest philosophical argument. There is no contradiction in the notion that both these 'uniformities' should be laws. But it is a most unwelcome conclusion.

There are three ways in which the Regularity theorist may attempt to evade this conclusion. The *first* is the most conservative from the point of view of the Naive Regularity theory. It is plausible, and indeed I think correct, to argue that it is a necessary condition for something being a law of nature that the objects about which the law holds should be nomically possible objects. There are no laws about things which the laws forbid to exist (other than that they cannot exist). It is also the case that, for everything which exists, that thing is not a centaur: $(x) (\sim Cx)$. That, however, is a Humean uniformity, and so a law. Admittedly, it is a Humean uniformity of a very special sort, a law whose statement involves only a single term (a law of universal scope), and that a negative term. One might well wonder whether a satisfactory theory of laws would want to treat this either as a law or a manifestation of a law. But the Naive Regularity view does not exclude it. Within this theory, it is a law. Hence centaurs are physically impossible. Combining this with our previous principle, that there are no laws about things which the laws forbid to exist other than that they cannot exist, there can be no laws about the properties that centaurs do or do not have.

The first point to be made about this solution is that, even if it succeeds, it serves to bring out how utterly devastating Kneale's argument from unrealized physical possibilities is when the Naive theory is not modified in any way. The argument of the previous paragraph has brought out that, from the standpoint of the unmodi-fied Naive theory, if something of a certain general sort does not exist omnitemporally, then it is physically impossible that it should exist. In fact, however, we believe that there are innumerable general sorts of thing which do not exist omnitemporally, but which are not ruled out by the laws of nature. In the particular case of centaurs it may be that they are physically impossible. They are physiologically unlikely beasts. But what applies to centaurs can hardly apply generally.

However, even if we abstract from the difficulty about unrealized physical possibilities, this first solution is unsatisfactory. The problem is that science wishes to recognize certain laws whose logical form the Regularity theorist seems forced to render as the conjunction of (x) $(\sim Fx)$ and (x) $(Fx \supset Gx)$. There can be true scien-tific generalizations about non-existent things. However, since this difficulty is also the fatal objection to the *second* attempt by a Regu-larity theorist to solve his present problem, I will postpone developing it for a moment.

This second attempt involves a modification of the Naive Regu-larity theory. This modification questions whether a formula like '(x) $(Fx \supset Gx)$' really captures the notion of a Humean uniformity. Perhaps the formula is too liberal, and it should be restricted by requiring the actual existence of Fs at some time:

$$(\exists x) \ (Fx) \ \& \ (x) \ (Fx \supset Gx).$$

In defence of this formula it may be said that uniformities without positive instances are really pseudo-uniformities.

To this it might be added that a uniformity such as (x) $(\sim Cx)$ does not satisfy anything but a formal criterion for existential import.

Things which are not centaurs do exist – they are everywhere – but a genuine uniformity must involve a positive antecedent. The notion of a positive antecedent is difficult to define, because a definition in terms of syntactically positive predicates is clearly insufficient. But the notion can be apprehended, and it is fairly clear that *not being a centaur* is semantically as well as syntactically a negative notion.

However, as already foreshadowed, the addition of a condition demanding that the antecedent exist is too strong. I have great sympathy with the insistence upon existential import. My feeling is that it is a basically sound reaction. It respects what Meinong so insultingly called 'a prejudice for the actual'. The laws of nature should concern only the actual behaviour of actual things. (An intuition which is one of the *admirable* intellectual sources of the Regularity theory.) Unfortunately, however, there are many cases where we assert the existence of laws but do not grant existence to the subject of the law. In the Regularity tradition these are often spoken of as 'vacuous' laws. But this is theory-laden terminology, deriving from such paradoxes as that about the centaurs with which we began this section. Since I think that a true theory of laws has no need to become entangled in these difficulties, I shall use a more neutral terminology and speak of *uninstantiated* laws. A number of examples may be cited.[4]

Newton's First Law. A case in point is Newton's First Law of Motion. The law-statement tells us what happens to a body which is not acted upon by a force. Yet it may be that the antecedent of the law is never instantiated. It may be that every body that there is, is acted upon by some force.

Foresight and prudence. One possible source of uninstantiated laws is the result of human foresight and prudence. W. E. Johnson gave the case of the brakeless trains (1924, Pt III, p. 12). It can be foreseen that brakeless trains would lead to accidents. As a result, all trains are fitted with brakes.[5] There are no brakeless trains. Hugh Mellor

---

[4] Molnar (1969, p. 84) gives as an example of an uninstantiated law:

Nothing travels faster than light.

But as David Lewis has pointed out to me, this seems not to be an example of an uninstantiated law at all. *Prima facie*, it is a law of universal scope involving a negation. Its apparent form is (x) $(\sim Fx)$, like the 'law' about there being no centaurs. To have an uninstantiated law we require the conjunction of (x) $(\sim Fx)$ with (x) $(Fx \supset Gx)$.

[5] A note for train enthusiasts. David Lewis tells me that there may have been brakeless trains. He says that early mineral trains had high friction axleboxes, went very slowly, and were very unsafe by our standards.

(1974, p. 167) gives the more contemporary, and perhaps better, example of precautions taken at a nuclear power station. It may be foreseen, as a matter of nomic truth, that, if a certain eventuality occurs, the result will be a certain sort of nuclear accident. We therefore try to ensure that this eventuality never occurs. We may be lucky enough to succeed. If so, the law governing this eventuality may be an uninstantiated one.

Functional laws. We now come to a very important possible source of uninstantiated laws. As was apparently first pointed out by C. D. Broad (1935; pp. 174–5 in the 1968 reprint), functional laws may give rise to uninstantiated laws. He points out that laws of the form $Q = f(P)$, with Q and P variable magnitudes, may involve missing values of P. Suppose, for instance, that P can take continuum-many values. It may well be that, omnitemporally, certain of the values are never instantiated. (The nomic equivalent of Hume's missing shade of blue.) Yet the functional law gives us the value of dependent Q for uninstantiated values of P as much for the instantiated values.

Perhaps all empirically plausible cases of uninstantiated laws reduce to cases of missing values of functional laws. Newton's First Law appears to reduce to an uninstantiated case of the Second Law, which is in turn a functional law. The 'law' governing brakeless trains is derivable from various functional laws governing masses in motion in an earth-like context. A plausible concrete scenario for Mellor's nuclear accident case would involve functional laws of physics.

Michael Tooley (1977) has argued that there are other logically possible cases of uninstantiated laws of a sort different from those given in this section. We will consider his cases in Chapter 8. But the cases already mentioned show that the Regularity theory cannot simply deny the existence of uninstantiated laws. Since it also cannot admit them promiscuously, some way must be found to admit them in a selective fashion.

The *third* alternative for a Regularity theorist is to admit uninstantiated laws, but only to admit them as a special case. The first-class or central cases of laws are instantiated laws. This respects the 'prejudice for the actual'. Uninstantiated laws are admitted only where they round out the system of instantiated uniformities, giving that system greater simplicity than it would have without the uninstantiated uniformities. (A functional law with 'missing values' is not so simple as a law where these values are not treated as missing.)

I think that this is undoubtedly the best strategy for a Regularity theorist. However, it demands a certain sophistication of the Regularity theory, a sophistication to be examined in Chapter 5, Section 4. There the whole project of defending the Regularity theory by putting 'systematic' restrictions upon the uniformities admitted as laws will be examined.

3

Critique of the Regularity theory (2)

In the previous chapter we saw that there are innumerable Humean uniformities which we are unwilling to account laws of nature or manifestations of laws of nature. Being a Humean uniformity is not sufficient for being a law of nature. The Naive Regularity theory is therefore false. The Regularity theorist must find some way to distinguish between Humean uniformities which are laws and those which are not, without compromising the spirit of the Regularity theory.

In this chapter we will investigate cases, or possible cases, where laws of nature exist but Humean uniformities are lacking. Clearly, they pose a potentially still more serious threat to the Regularity theory. In the last two sections of the chapter we will consider cases where there is a failure of correspondence between the content of the law and the content of its manifestation.

1 SPATIO-TEMPORALLY LIMITED LAWS

From time to time it is suggested by philosophers and scientists that the laws of nature may be different in different places and times. Obviously, this is not just the suggestion that the same sort of thing may behave differently in different sorts of conditions. The latter is compatible with the laws of nature being omnitemporally uniform. The suggestion is rather that the same sorts of thing may behave differently at different places and times, although the conditions which prevail are not different *except* in respect of place and time.

One philosopher who held such a view was Whitehead. He believed that the laws of nature might be different in different 'cosmic epochs'. (See 1933, Ch. 7, Sec. 5. Further references are given in Beauchamp 1972.)

As Michael Tooley has pointed out to me, however, there are two possibilities which can be distinguished here. It might be that,

24

although irreducibly different laws obtain in different cosmic epochs, these laws are governed by a single second-order law. This second-order law determines that, for any time t, if the laws at time t are L, then, given a time $g(t)$ which is a certain function of t, the laws at $g(t)$ will be a certain function, f, of L. The second possibility is that there is no such higher-order law. It is the second possibility which most clearly poses problems for the Regularity theory, and is the possibility which I wish to consider.

Two questions arise. (1) Is it possible for scientific laws to vary in this arbitrary way from one place and time to another? (2) Is the Regularity theorist well placed to deny that it is a possibility?

My initial inclination was to hold that (1) is not a possibility. If laws of nature are relations of universals, as I shall be arguing in the latter half of this book, it seems not to be a possibility. However, a case of Michael Tooley's, to be discussed in the next section, suggests that laws which essentially involve particulars must be admitted as a logical possibility. If so, the possibility of arbitrarily different laws in different cosmic epochs will have to be allowed, and the theory of laws modified to admit the possibility.

But whatever we say about (1), it does seem clear that the Regularity theorist is in a weak position to resist the suggestion that there can be such spatio-temporally limited laws.

The reason for this is that only a rather small conceptual gap separates cosmic, that is, Humean, uniformities from large-scale uniformities which are less than cosmic. Suppose that there are no cosmic uniformities at all, but that there are large-scale regularities of the sort we are envisaging. This supposition is logically compatible with all our observational evidence. How should the Regularity theorist describe the situation? 'There are no laws, but there are large-scale regularities' or 'There are laws, but they do not have cosmic scope'? The latter seems far closer to the pragmatic and positivist spirit which animates the Regularity analysis.

It seems, then, that the Regularity theory ought to be modified to allow the possibility of laws which are less than Humean uniformities. This, of course, exposes the theory to the paradox of the heap. Where, in the gamut of possible cases, do laws of limited scope end and merely accidental collocations begin? Presumably it will have to be said that there is no conceptually sharp dividing line. Laws fade off into states of affairs which are not laws.

I do not want to say that this consequence is, by itself, any fatal blow to the Regularity theory. But consideration of cosmic epochs and the like does give the theory a little nudge towards anti-Realism. What constitutes a law of nature becomes a bit more arbitrary and conventional.

2 LOCAL UNIFORMITIES AS LAWS

Worse follows. It seems logically possible that even a small-scale, local, possibility could be a law or manifestation of a law. Michael Tooley (1977) gives a fanciful case:

All the fruit in Smith's garden at any time are apples. When one attempts to take an orange into the garden, it turns into an elephant. Bananas so treated become apples as they cross the boundary, while pears are resisted by a force that cannot be overcome. Cherry trees planted in the garden bear apples, or they bear nothing at all. If all these things were true, there would be a very strong case for its being a law that all the fruit in Smith's garden are apples. And this case would be in no way undermined if it were found that no other gardens, however similar to Smith's in all other respects, exhibited behaviour of the sort just described. (p. 686)

Tooley is aware, of course, that one might try to counter such a case by suggesting that the garden has some property, P, such that it is a law that *all* gardens with property P behave in this way. (It might be the case that Smith's garden is the only actual garden with this property.) But what, Tooley asks, if (a) thousands of years of careful investigation of Smith's garden fails to differentiate it from other gardens; and (b) no experimental attempt to produce another garden for which the apple-generalization holds is ever successful? Would it not be rather reasonable to conclude that no such property P exists? The law would then be a limited or local law: essentially a law about Smith's garden.

The fanciful nature of the case need not detain us. Nothing turns upon it. We could suppose instead that uranium found in Australia behaves in a slightly different manner from uranium found elsewhere, but does not differ from other uranium in any of its identifying quantum-mechanical and other properties.

Still more realistic candidates for local uniformities which are nevertheless manifestations of laws are to be found in cosmological systems which make the universe spatially finite and then give the centre of the universe a special nomic role. The laws of nature were once thought to involve such a centre. It does not seem that such a system is involved in logical error about the nature of law.

26

However, I wish to emphasize particularly cases like Smith's garden and the uranium case. If cases like these are admitted then the Naive Regularity is refuted, and, I think, any Regularity theory is in serious trouble.

In the Smith's garden case as described by Tooley all sorts of things were imagined to have happened *which constituted objective tests of the law*. But surely it is possible for a law to hold, but for the circumstances which would constitute objective tests of the law never to occur? If so, why should there not be laws of purely local sort where, it so happens, objective tests were lacking? Nature, or we, failed to carry out any relevant experiments.

For instance, why might it not have been a *law* that, in a certain room, over a certain fixed time, everybody in the room had shoes on? Nobody submitted the law to objective test by trying to take their shoes off, but if they had tried, they would not have succeeded. Admittedly, we have no reason to think that such a law obtained. But might it not have obtained for all that?

These considerations, if admitted, are absolutely fatal for a Naive Regularity theory of law. The theory cannot claim that every local uniformity is a law. That would be madness. But if some *untested* local uniformities can be laws, how is the theory to mark off those local uniformities which are laws from those which are not? It is fairly clear, furthermore, that the difficulty is a most serious one for any sophistication of the Regularity theory.

The consolation for the Regularity theorist is that the objection, if successful, seems to refute not only the Regularity theory but also any other theory of the nature of laws of nature which has been proposed. Certainly it refutes the view that laws of nature must be in every case relations of universals. However, the Regularity theorist cannot comfort himself too deeply. The situation is not symmetrical. As will be seen later, the theory that laws of nature are relations between universals can be generalized to admit cases like that of Smith's garden, even if generalized in what I find a rather unintuitive way. No such generalization is available to the Regularity theory.

3 INFINITELY QUALIFIED LAWS

It might be a law that Fs are Gs, except where Fs have the further property H. In this exceptional case the law fails. It might even be the case that it is actually nomically impossible for FHs to be G. H might inhibit an F from being a G.

The case may now be made more complex. Suppose that there is another property, J, quite distinct from H, and that, although in general it is a law that Fs are Gs, it is not a law that FHs or FJs are Gs.

We are now prepared for a still more extreme possibility:

It is a law that Fs are Gs, except where Fs are Hs, are Js, and Ks . . . and so on for an *infinite* set of distinct properties.

It seems that there could be a law of this form. How will a Regularity theory deal with it?

Such a law will manifest itself in the following way (ignoring complications about uninstantiated Fs):

All Fs are Gs, except that there are FHs which are not Gs, FJs which are not Gs, FKs which are not Gs, and so on for an infinite set of distinct properties.

Can this be considered a uniformity? It is not a uniformity of the sort originally envisaged by the Regularity theory.

It is, of course, natural to seek for some single property, P, which underlies the infinite set {H, J, K . . .}, such that any particular having a property drawn from this set has P, and such that having both F and P ensures that the F is not a G. But it is possible that there is no such underlying property. It is logically possible that Fs naturally tend to be Gs, but that the tendency can be blocked by infinitely many quite different sorts of factor.

While a situation of this sort is not a paradigm case of a uniformity, it can perhaps be accommodated by stretching the definition of a Humean uniformity a little. For that reason, like the problem about regularities which do not persist beyond cosmic epochs, the possibility of infinitely qualified laws does not by itself refute the Regularity theory unless the latter is rather strictly conceived. But it may be noted that the possibility of such laws forces the Regularity theorist, and others, to distinguish sharply between laws and *statements* of law. Here are possible laws which, if they hold, can never actually be stated in full. Must not these laws, and so by implication all laws, be distinguished from statements of law? The possibility of infinitely qualified laws requires a Realist theory of the nature of laws. (Though not, just from this, a Realism about universals.)

28

Other patterns of infinite qualification seem possible. Suppose it to be nomically true that, in general, Fs are Gs, but that it is not a law that Fs which are Hs are Gs. Indeed, it is nomically true that Fs which are Hs are, in general, not Gs. This, however, is merely in general. It is nomically true that Fs which are Hs and Js are, in general, Gs. This however is merely in general. It is nomically true that Fs which are Hs and Js and Ks . . . It seems clear that such a progression of interfering factors, each interfering with the operation of the previous interfering factor, might go to any finite depth. But is it not also possible that the progression of interfering factors may have no end?

This second sort of case, however, is not so troublesome for a Regularity theory. For at each stage of the regress there is a finitely stateable uniformity. All Fs which are not Hs are Gs. All Fs which are Hs and are not Js are not Gs. And so on.

4 PROBABILISTIC LAWS

The considerations advanced in the first and third sections of this chapter, those from cosmic epochs and infinitely qualified laws, do not strike deeply at the Regularity theory, although they are important from the standpoint of the general theory of law. The argument of Section 2, that purely local uniformities might be laws or manifestations of laws, if successful, refutes the Naive Regularity theory. But that difficulty threatens to be a difficulty for any alternative theory also. The difficulty now to be considered poses quite special difficulties for the *Regularity* theory.

If we are to accept the interim verdict of contemporary physics, then many of the fundamental laws of nature issue not in regularities, but rather in probabilistic distributions.

What makes such a distribution the manifestation of a probabilistic law? It is not enough that there is a certain probability that an F be a G. For instance, it is not enough that there be a certain probability (>0, <1) that a uranium atom will disintegrate in a certain time. A probability of this sort is necessary for a probabilistic law but is not sufficient. For the facts given are compatible with the following further factors. Suppose that there is a property, D, which some but only some uranium atoms come to have. Suppose further that if a uranium atom comes to have D, then after an interval t it will disintegrate, but not otherwise. We can then speak of the probability that an (unspecified) uranium atom will disintegrate after interval t has elapsed, a probability dependent upon the relative frequency with which such atoms acquire property D. But no probabilistic law of disintegration is involved. The law is *deterministic*. For a probabilistic law, there must be no such differentiating factor D which determines the outcome. The law must be *irreducibly* probabilistic.

However, an irreducibly probabilistic law will not, in general, manifest itself in a Humean uniformity. Or, at any rate, it will not manifest itself in any ordinary Humean uniformity. We will consider shortly the suggestion that it manifests itself in a uniformity involving objective single-case propensities.

How might the Naive Regularity theory be adjusted to deal with probabilistic laws? Suppose it to be an (irreducibly) probabilistic law that Fs have a certain probability of being G. Consider in turn the case where the omnitemporal number of the Fs is finite, and the case where that number is infinite.

Taking the finite case first, the natural first move for a Regularity theorist is to identify the probabilistic law with the actual relative frequency of Gs among the Fs. However, this at once creates the spectre of a huge unwanted mass of probabilistic 'laws'. Suppose, for instance, that the universe is spatio-temporally finite. Wherever a general property is found sometimes in association with another property, and sometimes not, and there is no further differentiating property present which marks off the positive from the negative cases, there, the Regularity theorist will be forced to say, we have a probabilistic law. The law's content will be given by the relative frequency of the positive to negative cases.

If instead the class of Fs is infinite in number, then the notion of a relative frequency is not straightforwardly applicable. But the more sophisticated notion of a *limiting* relative frequency can be introduced. The notion of a random sequence is first defined, the technicalities of which need not be discussed here. Now if, in a random sequence of Fs, the frequency of Gs among Fs tends towards a certain fixed limit as the sequence of Fs becomes longer, that limit may be taken to be the relative frequency of Gs among Fs.

The existence of random sequences of Fs requires definite conditions which may not obtain. As a result, the notion of a limiting relative frequency is a more restrictive notion than that of relative frequency for finite classes. Hence there will not be the same worry about too many laws which we noticed in the finite case. It is therefore tempting for the Regularity theorist to try to introduce the notion of a limiting relative frequency even where the class of Fs is finite. In the finite case, the probability of a G being an F is identified with the limiting relative frequency of Gs among Fs which would obtain if, contrary to fact, the class of Fs were infinite.

This suggestion appears to be a classic case of the misuse of counterfactuals. What sort of truth-maker, what sort of ontological ground, can be provided for such counterfactuals? What states of affairs make these counterfactuals true? If one were developing a theory of laws as relations between universals, then perhaps we might appeal here to relations holding between the universals F and G. But the Regularity theorist has only the actual Fs, finite in number, a proportion of which are Gs. What here can determine a hypothetical limiting relative frequency one way or another? The counterfactual floats on nothing.

But even if we are dealing with genuine infinite collections, the probability given by a probabilistic law cannot be identified with the limiting relative frequency of a random infinite sequence. For each instantiation of a law is an independent event, uninfluenced by the other instantiations of the law. Since what happens on any particular occasion may be improbable, it is possible (and this means *physically* possible) that what happens even in the longest run should be improbable. It is possible therefore, physically possible, that the limiting relative frequency of Gs among the infinite class of Fs be such-and-such a figure, and yet this frequency fail to reflect the probabilities given by the law. Such a state of affairs is indefinitely improbable, but it is not impossible. (It is worth remembering here, as David Lewis has reminded me, that, whatever the actual nature of the infinite sequence is, however orderly, it too is indefinitely improbable.)

The point is that probabilistic laws appear to permit *any distribution at all* of the factors which they govern. Some distributions are vastly more probable than others, and the laws give these probabilities. But no distribution is impossible. Hence a probabilistic law cannot be identified with a limiting relative frequency. *A fortiori*, probabilistic laws cannot be identified with ordinary relative frequencies.

The fact is that probabilistic laws, if they are admitted, seem to point to something which no Regularity theory can accept: the failure of laws of nature to be logically supervenient upon particular matters of fact. For the Regularity theorist, if we are given the whole history and geography of the universe, that is, what happens at each particular place and time independently of what happens elsewhere, then the laws of nature are automatically given also. For laws are simply molecular facts of uniformity which collect these atomic facts. They are not anything over and above the atomic facts.

Probabilistic laws, however, cannot be handled in this way. For they cannot be identified with molecular facts about distributions, whether for finite or infinite cases. Probabilistic laws *permit* distributions which do not reflect the probabilities involved. They are therefore not logically supervenient upon, they are logically independent of, particular matters of fact. *Prima facie,* probabilistic laws cannot be accommodated by the Regularity theory.

A spectacular yet plausible case where the gap is discernible between law and manifestation is this. The law assigns a very high probability, which is nevertheless less than 1, to an F being G. The number of Fs is relatively small, but, as it happens, each F is a G. Given the right numbers, this may even be the most probable manifestation. Yet the law which is thus manifested in a uniformity is not a deterministic one.

It might be wondered what reasons we would have in such a situation to postulate a probabilistic rather than a deterministic law. But, as Tooley has pointed out (1977, p. 669), such reasons could easily exist. Suppose F to be a very rare sort of particle, created only occasionally in very special conditions. Suppose also that in the case of other, more common, particles, there is clear evidence that their behaviour is governed by non-deterministic laws assigning a certain high probability. Considerations of symmetry might strongly suggest that the F→G law also assigns no more than the same high probability to the F being G.

There is, however, a way in which the Regularity theorist can avoid all these difficulties and reduce probabilistic laws to uniformities, though it involves a considerable price. The solution is indicated by D. H. Mellor (1980, p. 106) who writes:

A law says that *all* things or events of some kind have a certain property or are related in a certain way to something else. If the law is statistical, the property is having a chance of having some property or of being related to something else.

What Mellor has done here, as I understand him, is to introduce into his ontology an irreducibly new, higher-level, sort of property: a chance of having an ordinary, lower-level property. These new properties attach to individual things. If there is a probabilistic law that Fs have a certain probability of being Gs, then it is a Humean uniformity that each F has the further property of having a certain chance, C, of being a G. In this way, the logical supervenience of laws upon the particular historical facts is restored. But particular facts now include the possession by particulars of these new sorts of property: objective chances.

One question which immediately arises for a Regularity theorist who accepts this account of probabilistic laws is whether he wishes to generalize it to apply to deterministic laws. Once probabilistic laws, however construed, are admitted, it is natural to reconstrue deterministic laws as a limiting case of probabilistic laws: those cases where the probability is one.[1] But if the deterministic laws are limiting cases of probabilistic laws, and if probabilistic laws involve higher-level properties (chances of having an ordinary property) then deterministic laws will involve higher-level properties also: chance 1 of having an ordinary property. Chance 1 leads us back to the old notion of a power. If it is a law that Fs are Gs, this involves Fs having two further properties. First, they have the power (chance 1) that necessitates that they be Gs. Second, they are Gs. With mere probabilistic laws, the (lesser) chance is also always present, but, since the chance is not always realized, the second property may not always be present.

In the case of deterministic laws, there will be a logically necessary connection holding *in re* between the power and its actualization. For probabilistic laws there can be no necessary con-

---

[1] Some care is needed here. It is necessary to distinguish between probability 1, and a probability indefinitely close to 1, that is, only infinitesimally different from 1. Suppose that the number of Fs is infinite, Fs are in general Gs, but a finite number of Fs are not Gs. The limiting relative frequency of Gs among Fs is then 1. As we have seen, this limiting frequency cannot be identified with the probability assigned by the law. Nevertheless, we may wish to say that it is a law that the probability of such an F being a G is 1. However, unlike the case of a deterministic law, we must add that, strictly, the value is 1 minus an infinitesimal. (For the new mathematics of infinitesimal probability, see for instance, Skyrms, 1980, Appendix 4.)

It is to be noted also, as pointed out by David Lewis, that if objective chances are introduced, as Mellor introduces them, then it would be possible for the relative frequency of Gs among the Fs to be *strictly* 1, and yet for the chance of an F being a G to be less than 1, including infinitesimally less, i.e. for the law not to be deterministic.

nection, because the chance may not be realized. But it is of the essence of the chance that it establishes a probability that the chance will be realized. It seems that we must think of it as a logical probability holding *in re*.

It is to be noticed that these powers and chances are *bare* powers and chances. Their nature seems exhausted in their manifestations. There is no possibility of identifying them, as a result of *a posteriori* investigation, with, say, a categorical structure, S̄, in the things which are F. For, in the case of genuinely probabilistic laws, this will simply be to replace the law that Fs have a certain probability of being G with the law that Ss have a certain probability of being G. Ss will then have to be accompanied by chances of being a G, thus reproducing the problem. I do not even think that we can identify one chance with another. Suppose that Fs have chance C_1 of being G, and chance C_2 of being H. Could these chances be the very same property? It does not seem so. It is the essence of the first property that it gives chance C_1 of being a G, and not of its essence that it gives chance C_2 of being an H. The same holds in reverse for the second property. So they cannot be identical. There is no question therefore of the one single property being responsible for a multitude of effects, a pattern to be found in much fruitful theoretical postulation.

It is to be noted, however, that chances are properties which can exclude each other. It is impossible that a certain object at a certain time should have two different chances of being a G. They form a set of determinates under a determinable, excluding each other by logical necessity.

I am inclined to think that the notion of a property which can only be described in itself as that which gives a certain chance of having an ordinary, first-level, property is an incoherent notion. But even if this is not so, the postulation of such properties seems an undesirable piece of metaphysics unless very strongly motivated. The defence of the battered Regularity theory hardly constitutes such a motive, especially since the postulation will suffice to deal with exactly *one* of the many difficulties faced by the theory.

It is to be noted, in any case, how far this solution to the problem of probabilistic laws has drifted from the original inspiration of the Regularity theory. Part of the rhetorical stock-in-trade of a Regularity theorist, handed down, of course, from Hume, consists of scornful reference to those who postulate connections between things and/or events which are anything more than mere uniformities. The connections are variously stigmatized as mysterious, unobservable, unknowable and unintelligible. (Mellor following Ramsey (1978), attacks the idea of laws of nature as relations between universals in just this way. See his 1980, p. 124.) Yet a theorist who feels himself free to introduce objective chances as properties of particular things and/or events should surely be a little bit careful about what ontological theories he finds mysterious and unintelligible. He is living in an ontological glass house.

5 PROBABILISTIC LAWS: THE RETREAT TO POSITIVISM

However, for those who wish to give an account of probabilistic laws within the framework of the Regularity theory, but who spurn objective single-case chances, there is another option. It is represented by J. L. Mackie (1974, Ch. 9) and Brian Skyrms (1980). The idea is to identify the law with the evidence which, if we could have it, would persuade us that we were in the presence of a probabilistic law.
Mackie writes:

If radium atoms are considered in one or other possible series, for instance a series determined by increasing distance at time t_1 from some arbitrarily chosen point, their decaying or not decaying within some period of time may exhibit the sort of pattern that makes a series look as if it were a random collective approaching a certain limiting frequency. Its doing this, I suggest, would constitute the holding of a statistical law of working, (p. 240)

A statistical law, then, must consist in some outcome's having some limiting frequency in certain actual series or sequences of instances of the assemblage of antecedent conditions. (p. 241)

. . . . long runs of such instances in various spatio-temporally determined series usually exhibit frequencies close to the limiting one. (p. 241)

What may be thought of as a sophistication of this approach is to be found in Skyrms, although he says that his central notion is not essentially tied to limiting relative frequencies. The notion is that of a *resilient* probability. Suppose that there is a certain probability of an F being a G. For this to be a *resilient* probability it is further necessary that this probability remain the same over suitable subclasses of F. Fs that are J, that are K, that are L . . . have the same probability of being a G that the original class of the Fs had.

35

When this idea is applied to the giving of a Regularity account of probabilistic laws, we have the condition that Gs have a certain limiting frequency among the Fs, and that, as we vary the attendant circumstances of the Fs, the limiting frequency of Gs is maintained, in each class of attendant circumstances.[2]

The first point to be noted about this approach is that it introduces a considerable arbitrary and conventional element into the account of probabilistic laws. The law-*statement* assigns a precise probability of an F being a G. But, according to these views, this conceals the fact that there will regularly be an element of decision that the facts are to be so described.

Mackie and Skyrms are honest men and do not conceal the point. Mackie says of his own remarks about the law concerning radium atoms:

This statement may well seem crude. But this is deliberate. It is all too easy in this area to sacrifice reality to precision. (p. 240)

Skyrms says:

The only sort of physical randomness that makes sense, then, is randomness relative to a given set of physical properties. (There is no *absolute* physical randomness. There is no *absolute* resiliency.) (p. 15)

And again:

Things are not so clear-cut as one might hope. We find no absolute resiliency in physics, nice as it would be if we did. And philosophers have no business trying to lay down, a priori, standards for the scope of resiliency appropriate to physical theories. Standards for resiliency evolve along with physical theory in a big virtuous circle, and in our dealings with nature we take what we can get. (p. 19)

It is clear, I think, why Skyrms has to be content with imprecision and relativity. His notion of resiliency seems an important and illuminating one when thinking about what constitutes the objective tests of a law. But it appears that we should demand no more of *laws themselves* than this: that they should be *potentially* resilient. If it really is a law that Fs have probability P of being Gs, then Fs have this probability *under every nomically possible circumstance.*

---

[2] In private communication from Skyrms, received late in the composition of this work, he disclaims the intention, which his text suggested to me, of using the notion of resiliency to cast light on the truth-conditions for statements of law. However, an ontological interpretation of his work still seems interesting in its own right.

But that all these circumstances sometimes obtain is contingent. We expect that some will never obtain. To the extent that the circumstances are varied, either by nature or by our deliberate design, to that extent there may be confirmation available that the law holds.

Skyrms, however, because he is a Regularity theorist, has only available to him the actual occasions of variation, and so has to make resiliency over these occasions constitutive of the law. The spottiness of the occasions of variation accounts for the spottiness of his concept of a law.

In fact, however, it is easy to conceive of there being probabilistic laws for which neither nature nor art has provided a test. Suppose that Gs have a certain limiting frequency among the Fs, and that this frequency is resilient over a wide range of factors. But suppose that, omnitemporally, Fs are Hs, and Js and Ks. Are these further factors nomically relevant to an F being a G? It seems that they might be or that they might not be, and that this is a question with an objective answer, although, as things stand, there might be no evidence available which epistemically probabilified any answer. Skyrms, however, would have to treat this as a case where there was no objective matter of fact to be decided.

Mackie's position, I take it, falls with that of Skyrms, unless, indeed, he is advocating that we count as a probabilistic law something even less ontologically precise than Skyrms' resilient relative frequencies. But then his position would seem to collapse back into treating probabilistic laws as constituted by mere relative frequency.

6 FUNCTIONAL LAWS

We have seen in the case of probabilistic laws that the content of the law does not determine uniquely the nature of the manifestation, nor does the manifestation determine uniquely the content of the law. The latter phenomenon can also occur in the case of functional laws.

We have already considered the possibility that a functional law might hold, but that there might be missing, that is, uninstantiated, values of the function (Ch. 2, Sec. 7). Suppose now that a functional law appears to hold, but that the instantiated values of the function do not suffice to determine the function uniquely. Many possible functions, perhaps infinitely many, are logically compatible with the instantiated values.

37

The difficulty for the Naive Regularity theory is this. It seems natural to think that, although many possible functions are compatible with the data, there is in fact just one function which constitutes the law which actually governs the situation. But the relevant set of Humean uniformities do not logically determine what that function is.

Indeed, as Timothy Potts (then a student at Sydney University) pointed out, given the Naive Regularity theory *each* function which fits the instantiated values will come out as a Humean uniformity, and thus as a law. Yet can they all be laws? The corresponding law-statements will sustain logically incompatible counterfactuals. Given that the missing values are nomically possible ones, as they well may be, this, *contra* the Naive Regularity theory, makes the possible laws incompatible with each other.

It appears that a more sophisticated Regularity theory will have to choose one of the possible functions on the basis of simplicity and coherence. We are to take as 'the' law whatever function gives us the simplest fit for the instantiated values and/or the greatest coherence with other functional laws.

This, however, creates the possibility that the nature of the function, and thus the law, will have to be settled in an arbitrary manner. Suppose that the universe appears to involve only three fundamental laws, all functional laws. Two of the apparent laws, L_1 and L_2, which do not involve any uninstantiated values, differ in their mathematical properties, but are equally simple. An apparent third law, L_3, has uninstantiated values, and furthermore the uninstantiated values are compatible with two fairly simple mathematical functions. The first function resembles the L_1 function, the second function resembles the L_2 function. What *is* the L_3 law? An arbitrary choice will have to be made.

The drift towards convention and subjectivity, which tends to occur wherever the Naive Regularity theory has to be modified, continues.

4

Critique of the Regularity theory (3)

It was argued in Chapter 2 that there are innumerable Humean uniformities which we think are neither laws of nature nor manifestations of such laws. In Chapter 3 it was argued that there are, or can be, laws of nature which are not manifested in Humean uniformities. It was also pointed out that in the case of probabilistic and functional laws the relation between the content of a law and the content of the manifestation of the law need not be identity, yet identity is demanded by the Regularity theory.

In this chapter, all these difficulties will be waived. Suppose it to be a law of nature that Fs are Gs, and that this law issues in the (actually instantiated) uniformity that each F is a G. Even given this favourable case for the Regularity theorist, there are great difficulties in identifying the law and the uniformity.

1 LACK OF INNER CONNECTION

Suppose it to be a law that Fs are Gs, and suppose there to be a plurality of Fs. Consider one of these: *a*. By hypothesis, it is a G. We can say that *a*'s being F nomically necessitates *a*'s being G.

Suppose, however, that we consider this particular instance falling under the law from the standpoint of the Regularity theory. What does the theory postulate to obtain? Nothing but the two states of affairs: *a*'s being F, and *a*'s being G. Yet such a mere conjunction of states of affairs can obtain where there is absolutely no nomic connection between the states of affairs involved. For the Regularity theory, the essence of the nomic connection is not to be found in the two states of affairs and any dyadic relation which holds just between them. Rather, *a*'s being F nomically necessitates *a*'s being G only because *the other Fs* are also all of them Gs. That the conjunction of states of affairs is a case of nomic necessitation is a *purely relational property* of the conjunction.

The objection to the Regularity theory is that this seems not enough. We think that if a's being F is nomically to necessitate a's being G, then at least part of what must exist is some direct, dyadic relation holding between the two particular states of affairs. (This is part of what Hume was saying when he demanded a necessary connection between particular cause and particular effect over and above the fact that they instantiate a regularity.)

Suppose now that a is the only instance of an F in the whole history of the universe, and that it is still a G. In this case the Naive Regularity theory, at least, is forced to say that it is a law that Fs are Gs. a's being F necessitates a's being G. But this also is unintuitive. For it is natural to say that, given a is F and is G, and given that this is the only F, it is still a further question whether or not a relation of nomic necessitation holds between the two states of affairs.

2 LAWS OF NATURE AS PRINCIPLES OF EXPLANATION

Suppose that a number of Fs have all been observed, and that each is a G. No F that is not a G has been observed. We might ask for an explanation of this fact. One possible explanation is that it is a law that Fs are Gs. If such a law really holds, then the explanation will be quite a good one.

Suppose, however, that laws are mere regularities. We are then trying to explain the fact that all observed Fs are Gs by appealing to the hypothesis that all Fs are Gs. Could this hypothesis serve as an explanation? It does not seem that it could. That all Fs are Gs is a complex state of affairs which is in part *constituted* by the fact that all observed Fs are Gs. 'All Fs are Gs' can even be rewritten as 'All observed Fs are Gs and all unobserved Fs are Gs'. As a result, trying to explain why all observed Fs are Gs by postulating that all Fs are Gs is a case of trying to explain something by appealing to a state of affairs part of which is the thing to be explained. But a fact cannot be used to explain itself. And that all *unobserved* Fs are Gs can hardly explain why all observed Fs are Gs.

The point may be obscured because explanations are confused with *good reasons*. That all the observed Fs are Gs may well constitute a good reason for thinking that all Fs are Gs. But a good reason for P is not necessarily an explanation of P. The presence of smoke is a good reason for thinking that fire is present. But it is not an explanation of the presence of fire.

Laws, however, explain regularities.[1] Even if we take the Humean uniformity itself, that all Fs are Gs, it seems to be an explanation of this uniformity that it is a law that Fs are Gs. But, given the Regularity theory, this would involve using the law to explain itself. We need to put some 'distance' between the law and its manifestation if the law is to explain the manifestation.

It is possible, of course, to reject the idea that laws of nature are principles of explanation. Wittgenstein said in the *Tractatus* (1921):

The whole modern conception of the world is founded on the illusion that the so-called laws of nature are the explanations of natural phenomena. (6.371)

But surely, all things being equal, we should prefer an account of laws which makes appeals to them genuine explanations?

3 THE PARADOXES OF CONFIRMATION

The line of argument in this section will be this. If we are concerned with the confirmation of statements of unrestricted, universally quantified, material implication – that is to say, with statements of Humean uniformities – then the 'paradoxes' are not genuinely paradoxical. It does not follow, however, that the paradoxes pose no difficulty for the view that laws of nature are mere Humean uniformities. For that to be the case, it is necessary that they not be paradoxical with respect to the confirmation of such statements as 'It is a law of nature that Fs are Gs'. Otherwise, statements of mere Humean uniformity will have a property which statements of purported laws of nature lack. Now, with regard to what has always been treated as the *central* paradox of confirmation, it is not clear that there is any asymmetry between 'It is a Humean uniformity that Fs are Gs' and 'It is a law of nature that Fs are Gs'. But, I will argue, if we consider a further paradox, then an asymmetry emerges.

The paradoxes were discovered by Carl Hempel (1945). The traditional central difficulty arises thus. If we consider the generalization:

For all x, x is a raven $\supset x$ is black,

---

[1] In Part II a distinction will be drawn between underived laws and derived laws (Ch. 10, Sec. 3). Derived laws are nomic truths deductively derived from the set of underived laws. I do not think that derived laws explain regularities.

then, while the observation of a raven which is not black refutes the generalization, the observation of a raven which is black, although failing to establish the theory, would seem to confirm it. However, the generalization is logically equivalent to:

For all x, x is not black $\supset$ x is not a raven.

But if the observation of a black raven confirms the original statements, so, presumably, the observation of a non-black non-raven, for instance a white shoe, confirms the second statement. Yet it seems a reasonable assumption that what confirms the second statement also confirms the logically equivalent first statement. Hence the observation of a white shoe confirms that:

For all x, x is a raven $\supset$ x is black.

That is the paradox upon which attention has been focussed. But as Hempel realized, the generalization is also confirmed by observation of non-ravens which are black: observation of black shoes as well as white. For the generalization says something about everything that there is, *viz.* that either that thing is not a raven or, if it is a raven, then it is black. Hence, once an object is observed to be a non-raven, the observation confirms the generalization regardless of what colour the object turns out to have.

If we remember that we are dealing with a material implication, then there is nothing paradoxical here. It is simply a consequence of the truth-table for '$\supset$'. We could exhibit this by rewriting the generalization as:

For all x, $((x$ is a raven and x is black) v (x is not a raven and x is black) v (x is not a raven and x is not black)).

Instances of any one of the three disjuncts will do as confirmers. Indeed, at any rate if we abstract from any knowledge which we have about the frequency of ravens compared to non-ravens or black things to non-black things, it would seem that instantiations of the disjuncts are of equal value as confirmers.

Now, however, consider the hypothesis that it is a law of nature that Fs are Gs and take some individual, a. With respect to the properties F and G there are four possibilities concerning a:

(1) Fa & Ga
(2) Fa & ~Ga

(3) ~Fa & Ga

(4) ~Fa & ~Ga.

(I will call (1) and (2) the positive instances, (3) and (4) the negative instances. (2), although a positive instance, is a falsifying one.) It is natural to think that (1) confirms the law-hypothesis, it is clear that (2) refutes it. For reasons which will emerge, the status of (4) is ambiguous and so I shall leave it aside for the present. But what of (3)? *Prima facie*, if possibility (3) is realized, then the law-hypothesis is neither refuted *nor confirmed*. It is true that (3) refutes another hypothesis: that it is a law that Gs are Fs. But why should this be thought to confirm that it is a law that Fs are Gs?

But suppose, as the Naive Regularity view holds, that we can substitute '(x) (F$x \supset$ Gx)' for 'it is a law that Fs are Gs'. Then, because of the truth-table for '$\supset$', it follows that (3) will be a confirmer of the law along with (1) and (4). So '(x) (F$x \supset$ Gx)' cannot be substituted for 'it is a law that Fs are Gs'.

Following up this point, I believe that we can see *why* it is that (3) fails to confirm the law-hypothesis. As Dretske remarks (1977, p. 261), confirmation is roughly the converse of explanation. (I take him to be speaking here of the confirmation of hypotheses involving *laws*.) Suppose that we have no direct evidence bearing upon the hypothesis that it is a law that Fs are Gs. If we then come upon an object which is both an F and a G then this observation would be explained by the law-hypothesis. So it confirms the hypothesis. Again, if we come upon an object which is neither an F nor a G, then perhaps it can still be said that this observation is explained by the law-hypothesis. For, given the law, we know that since the object is not a G, it cannot be an F. But suppose, finally, that we come upon something that is not an F but is a G. There is no case at all for saying that this observation is explained by the hypothesis that it is a law that Fs are Gs. So it does not in any way confirm the law.

But, to what has been said so far, the following objection may be urged by a Regularity theorist. Law-statements at least entail the corresponding statement of Humean uniformity. From the premiss 'it is a law that Fs are Gs' the material conditional 'for all x, x is F $\supset x$ is G' may be deduced. But, as we have seen, along with Fs that are Gs, and non-Fs that are non-Gs, non-Fs that are Gs confirm the material conditional. Observation of non-Fs that are Gs must therefore confirm the law-statement.

However, this is a bad argument, and there is no reason to accept its conclusion. It is a false principle that where P entails Q, and R confirms Q, then R must confirm P. R may be so far from confirming P that it actually refutes P. That all mice are under three inches long entails that all mice are under three feet long. The discovery of a mouse two feet long would confirm the latter proposition but falsify the former.

One might try to restrict the principle by restricting R to propositions which are compatible with P. This is actually the situation in the case which we are concerned with. But even this restricted principle fails to hold. The existence of unicorns entails the existence of animals. The observation of a zebra, which is compatible with the existence of unicorns, not merely confirms the existence of animals but does better by establishing their existence. Yet the observation of zebras does nothing to confirm the existence of unicorns.

That completes my argument to show that one of the paradoxes of confirmation spells trouble for the Regularity theory. But I find an opportunity to cast some further light upon the theory of the confirmation of nomological statements.

Michael Tooley has drawn my attention to the following line of argument. Suppose it to be a law that Fs are Gs. Is it not then equally a *law* that non-Gs are non-Fs? But if the latter is a law, then non-Gs which are non-Fs are certainly confirming instances of the law. For they are 'positive instances' of the law. If observation of them does not confirm it, then nothing does. But if the observation confirms the law, then it confirms the logically equivalent law that Fs are Gs.

This argument is interesting because, if correct, it supplies a reason for thinking that observation of non-G non-Fs may confirm the F→G law, a reason which does not depend upon taking the law as a material implication. As a result, it does not have the consequence that non-Fs which are Gs are confirmers of the law. It drives a wedge between the two types of negative instance. Another wedge has already appeared with the earlier suggestion that the law explains why a non-G is a non-F in a way that it does not explain the observation of a non-F which is a G.

The argument suggested by Tooley, however, has an uncertain point. Should we allow the premiss that if it is a law that Fs are Gs, then it is a law that non-Gs are non-Fs? Perhaps all that should be admitted is that if it is a law that Fs are Gs, then it is *the case* that all non-Gs are non-Fs. And indeed, if laws of nature are relations between universals, as will be argued in Part II, and if there are no negative universals, as I am also inclined to argue, then it will not be a law that non-Gs are non-Fs. It is true that I draw a distinction between underived and derived laws (Ch. 10, Sec. 3), and, given that distinction, I allow it to be a *derived* law that non-Gs are non-Fs. But derived laws are supervenient upon underived laws: they are nothing but entailments of premises made up of true statements of underived laws.

If the statement that it is a law that Fs are Gs entails nothing more than that each non-G is a non-F, then the Tooley argument for thinking that observation of a non-G non-F confirms the law-hypothesis breaks down. We have also seen that to argue that because observation of a non-G non-F confirms the generalization that each non-G is a non-F, it therefore confirms the entailer of 'each non-G is a non-F', *viz.* 'it is a law that Fs are Gs', is to appeal to a false principle.

However, there does seem to be some reason to think that observation of a non-G non-F confirms in some way that it is a law that Fs are Gs. I am influenced particularly by the fact that the law seems to *explain* why all non-Gs are non-Fs. At the same time, however, Fs that are Gs seem better confirmers of the law than non-G non-Fs. I suggest that the situation is that observation of Fs which are Gs provides first-grade confirmation, observation of non-F non-Gs second-grade confirmation, and observation of non-F Gs no confirmation at all. Working out the suggestion will involve no appeal to such things as normal background knowledge.

Non-Gs have the following importance in testing the hypothesis that it is a law that Fs are Gs, or even the hypothesis that all Fs are Gs. Either they are Fs or they are non-Fs. If they are Fs, however, the hypotheses are falsified. Hence observation of a non-G non-F is a case where, as we may put it, the hypothesis was up for testing but was not falsified. 'Survival' of such tests is a point in favour of the hypothesis. Non-Fs, by contrast, have no such importance. Whether they are Gs or are non-Gs, the hypothesis survives.

I do not think that it matters that in the case of a non-G non-F we may become aware that it is a non-F before we realize that it is a non-G, and so lose interest in it as a potential falsifier. The class of non-Gs has a certain objective logical relation to the hypo-theses. The relation is that of being a class of potential falsifiers:

because if any of the non-Gs are Fs, then the hypothesis is falsified.

Second-grade confirmation, then, is failure to falsify, but failure to falsify in a context (the context of the non-Gs) which permits the possibility of falsification. The context of the Fs, of course, provides the same possibility. So an F which is a G provides second-grade confirmation also. The relative number of Fs by comparison with the non-Gs (intuitively, there are far fewer ravens than non-black things) may have a further influence here, normally tipping the balance towards the worth as confirmers of the positive instances.

But what of the special value as confirmers of observation of Fs which are Gs? What of first-grade confirmation? If we are concerned with mere universal generalizations, then I do not think that they do have a special value. (And, as we have seen, even observation of non-Fs which are Gs must be given some confirmatory value.) But given the right theory of law, a special value can plausibly be attached.

I shall be arguing in Part II that only the 'positive instantiations' of a law are genuine instantiations of the law. An F that is a G instantiates the law that Fs are Gs. Non-G non-Fs do not instantiate the law, because there are no such universals. As a result, in the positive instances there is something there to be explained: the conjunction of two properties. The confirmation of the law given by observation of the conjunction is therefore direct in a way that it is not in the negative cases. What we have in the negative cases taken by themselves is a mere Humean uniformity: a consequence of the law but not the law itself. Hence observation of FGs confirm the law in a way that observation of non-F non-Gs do not.

4 THE PROBLEM OF COUNTERFACTUALS

Law-statements support counterfactuals. If the law-statements are true, then the counterfactuals supported are said to be true. The statement that it is a law that Fs are Gs supports the counterfactual that if a, which is not in fact an F, were to be an F, then it would also be a G. If the law obtains, then this counterfactual is said to be true.

Statements of mere uniformity, however, do not support counterfactuals in this way. Suppose it to be a mere uniformity that everybody in a certain room at a certain time is wearing a wristwatch. There will be no particular reason to assert that if a, who was not in the room at the time, had been in the room, then *a* would have been wearing a wrist-watch.

Statements of Humean uniformity, however, are nothing more than statements of *unrestricted* or *cosmic* uniformity. How can this difference in scope, this setting the scene in the largest room of all, contribute anything to the support of counterfactuals? Laws, therefore, cannot be identified with mere uniformities.

Notice that it is not part of this argument that law-statements are the only sort of statement which support counter-factuals. All the soldiers in a certain place at a certain time may be in uniform. Furthermore, this may be no accident. Orders may have been given which ensure that soldiers who are in that place at that time are all in uniform. Under these circumstances, the counterfactual statement 'If soldier *a* had been in that place at that time, then he would have been wearing uniform' may well be accounted true. But it is not a law of nature that soldiers in that place at that time are wearing uniform.

It is very often the case that, when a counterfactual is said to be true, it is said to be true in virtue of some necessity, whether that necessity be logical, nomic or of some other sort. In the soldier case, it seems that it is only because there are laws governing human actions that the counterfactual can be asserted. Perhaps soldiers at that place and time wear uniform as a nomic effect of the issuing of certain orders. Nevertheless, the statement which supports the counterfactual is not a law of nature.

It is to be noticed also that, given a law-statement, there are definite limits to the range of individuals which can figure in the counterfactual statements sustained by the law-statement. Suppose that we have a law governing the interaction of pairs of electrons. We can imagine two electrons, E_1 and E_2, which do not exist, but still assert that, if they did exist, they would interact as provided for in the law. Suppose, again, that P is an actually existing proton and E an actually existing electron. We can assert that, if P were an electron, P and E would repel each other according to the electron-formula. We might make such an assertion in the course of developing an argument to show that P is not an electron. But now suppose P to be a certain quadratic equation or a certain philosopher. Can we still assert that, if P had not been a quadratic equation (a philosopher) but an electron, P and E would be governed by the electron-formula? It is not clear that we can. To suppose that an equation or a philosopher is an electron is to make such extraordinary suppositions that we are perhaps not entitled to think that, in these new worlds, the ordinary laws of physics will continue to hold.

It seems that we can say only this. If P were anything at all, including something which does not exist, and E an electron, then, for *most* or for *many* values of P, it can be asserted truly that, if P were an electron, it would repel E according to the electron-formula. This limited result, however, is amply sufficient to show that the electron-formula is not just a statement of a Humean uniformity. For the latter does not support counterfactuals *at all*.

The argument given so far refutes the suggestion that a law-statement supports a certain counterfactual if and only if the conjunction of the law-statement plus the antecedent of the counterfactual entails the truth of the consequent of the counter-factual. From the conjunction of the electron-formula, and the premiss that P (which is in fact a quadratic equation or a philosopher) is an electron, it follows that P obeys the electron-formula. Yet we have seen reason to doubt that the electron-formula sustains counterfactuals about what would hold if quadratic equations or philosophers were electrons. Again as Mackie has pointed out (1966), from a statement of mere uniformity, such as the statement that everybody in a certain room is wearing a wrist-watch, together with the statement that randomly chosen *a* is in the room (actually false), it follows that *a* is wearing a wrist-watch. Yet the statement of uniformity clearly does *not* support the counterfactual that if *a* were to be in the room, *a* would be wearing a wrist-watch.

It seems plausible, however, that, provided the antecedent of the counterfactual has been fully stated, the sort of entailment just illustrated is a *necessary* condition for a law-statement to support a counterfactual. Some further limiting condition is then required to give necessary and sufficient conditions for a law-statement to support counterfactuals.

Consider the case of the wrist-watch again. Suppose that in thought we add *a* to the persons in the room, although we know that *a* is in fact not in the room. We can see no particular reason to think that *a* will resemble the people actually in the room in respect of wearing a wrist-watch. This seems to be the reason why we do not think that the statement of uniformity sustains the counterfactual.

Suppose, again, that we are given an electron formula, and the false supposition that P, actually a quadratic equation or a philosopher, is an electron. The supposition that a quadratic equation (philosopher) is an electron is so extraordinary, we are so altering the world in making the supposition, that we have no particular reason to think that the electron-formula will hold in this altered world. So we do not think that the electron-formula can sustain a counterfactual involving P.

Suppose, finally, that 'all Fs are G' is a statement of Humean uniformity. If we suppose that a is an F, although in fact it is not an F, what reason have we to think that this new F will come within the scope of the uniformity? It may or it may not. The Humean uniformity is a molecular state of affairs. To suppose that a is also F is to suppose that the original molecular state of affairs is augmented by a further state of affairs: a's being F. What reason is there to think that it would also be augmented by a's being G?

But, by comparison, if it is a law that Fs are Gs, and if we suppose, what is false, that a is an F, and if the supposition that a is an F is not too radical, there will be no reason to think that the law fails to hold in the altered world. Hence the law-statement supports the counterfactual.

At this point, however, a difficulty raised by David Lewis should be considered. Suppose that Determinism is true. Determinists assert the truth of counterfactuals, and we do not think that they are inconsistent to do so. But when a Determinist supposes falsely that a is F, and then considers what consequence will follow from this supposition, is he not involved in inconsistency? For in the real world it is determined that a is not an F (or, if a is non-existent, it is determined that there is no a). Is a, then, to be F by a miracle? If so, the Determinist has also to suppose that Determinism is false. The implausible alternative is that the Determinist must covertly suppose that world-history is altered in whatever way may be necessary to bring it about that a is F.

I think that the answer to this is that the second alternative is not so implausible. In making such a counterfactual supposition, we feel ourselves free to tinker with particular states of affairs fairly much as we please. We are interested in what the laws, taken by themselves, dictate. Our false supposition must not be such as to call the laws into question: it must be a physically possible supposition. (Or, if physically impossible, we must be abstracting from whatever laws

49

make it physically impossible.) But it does not have to be physically possible relative to the laws *plus* actual history and geography.

In a counterfactual supported by laws, the laws call the tune. Why is this? I take it that it is because the laws involve something which the Regularity theory denies them to have, and which particular states of affairs do not have: a certain necessity (which need not be logical). They say what must happen, and so they have authority in counterfactual reasoning.

What has been done so far is this. (1) It has been pointed out that law-statements (in many cases) do, but statements of local and Humean uniformity in general do not, support counterfactuals. Laws are therefore not Humean uniformities. (2) A theory of what it is for a law-statement to support a counterfactual was sketched.[2] The law-statement plus the fully stated antecedent of the counterfactual must entail the consequent of the counterfactual. Furthermore, the supposition of the truth of the antecedent of the counterfactual must not be such as to bring into doubt whether, in this new thought-situation, the law continues to hold. It is the necessity of the law which then ensures the truth of the counterfactual. This seems to *explain* why statements of Humean uniformity do not sustain counterfactuals, and explain why law-statements do. So, again, laws are not simply Humean uniformities.

An important attempt to evade the above arguments has been made by Mackie (1966). Suppose that we have evidence which makes it *inductively very probable* that all Fs are Gs. We then consider an *a* which we know or believe not to exist, or not to be an F. On the supposition that *a* is an F, however, it is inductively very probable that *a* is a G. We are therefore entitled to assert that if *a* were to be an F, then it would be a G.

This point, neutral in itself, can then be used to show how Humean uniformities might support counterfactuals, and so be laws after all. The argument is very simple. When we actually assert the existence of a Humean uniformity, and further use the assertion to support counterfactuals, it will be because we think we have inductive evidence for the obtaining of this uniformity. Hence the counterfactual is justified.

The first thing to be said about this suggestion is something

---

[2] Notice that this is not put forward as a *general* theory of what it is for a statement to support a counterfactual. A unified general theory may be too much to hope for. At any rate, I have not sought to give one.

which Mackie himself points out. If the Regularity theorist is to take this way out of the problem of counterfactuals, then it must be possible to give a rational solution to the Problem of Induction *while assuming that the laws of nature are mere uniformities*. It is impossible to combine (1) Mackie's way out, (2) the Regularity theory of laws with (3) inductive scepticism. I believe, however, and will argue in the next section, that to accept a Regularity theory of laws is to be committed to inductive scepticism.

I have two other difficulties with Mackie's suggestion. First, if statements of laws of nature sustain counterfactuals in this manner, then the counterfactuals ought to inherit the uncertainty which attends inductive justification. Suppose that all the observed Fs are Gs, but that there is other evidence which counsels a little caution about whether it is a law that Fs are Gs. It would be rational to reason: on the basis of the evidence it is probable, but not certain, that it is a law that Fs are Gs. The appropriate counterfactual would appear to be: 'If *a* were to be an F, then it is very probable that *a* would be a G'. That is to say, the consequent of the counterfactual will be a statement of probability. (Or, if Mackie's account of counterfactuals as condensed arguments is correct, the conclusion of the argument will be a statement of probability.)

But, given these circumstances, I do not think that we would assert this counterfactual. Either it is a law that Fs are Gs, or it is not. If it is a law, then the counterfactual that is true is just 'If *a* were to be an F, then *a* would be a G'. If it is *not* a law, then, in default of other facts, the counterfactual is simply false. If Mackie is right, then counterfactuals of this sort should reflect our inductive uncertainties. But they seem not to do so. We do not assert a counterfactual with a probabilistic consequent. Rather, we assert a counterfactual with the strong consequent, but assert it in a suitably tentative manner.

The second objection is this. It seems logically possible that a rational creature should have knowledge (or at least true beliefs) about the content of some or all of the laws of nature, although that knowledge or belief was not inductively acquired or supported. Now might not such a creature use law-statements to support counterfactuals in just the same way that we do? It seems possible. Yet how would it be possible if the assertion of such counterfactuals involves reliance upon an inductive inference from antecedent to consequent?

51

I know of no other way besides Mackie's in which a Regularity theorist can hope to solve the problem for his analysis posed by the fact that law-statements sustain counter-factuals.

I will finish this section by mentioning a point put to me by Chris Mortensen in correspondence. The traditional difficulty for the Regularity theory which we have been exploring is this. If it is a law that Fs are Gs, then it will often be the case that we wish to assert that if *a*, which is not an F, had been an F, then it would have been a G. But a mere regularity cannot sustain such counterfactuals. Here is Mortensen's new difficulty. Suppose instead that we consider an actual F which is a G. Will we not often be prepared to assert that if this thing had not been a G then it would not have been an F? If it had not expanded, then it would not have been a metal. But can the Regularity theorist give an account of such counterfactuals? Why assume that the regularity would have been maintained if the object had not been a G? Why not instead assume that if the thing had not been a G, it would still have been an F, and the regularity (law) would have failed?

5 THE PROBLEM OF INDUCTION

In this section it will be argued that if laws of nature are nothing but Humean uniformities, then inductive scepticism is inevitable. The argument has its complications, so it may be advisable to begin by sketching its course.

I start from the premiss that ordinary inductive inference, ordinary inference from the observed to the unobserved, is, although *invalid*, nevertheless a rational form of inference. I add that not merely is it the case that induction is rational, but it is a necessary truth that it is so.

To say that the rationality of induction is a necessary truth does not, of course, absolve us from saying why it is a necessary truth. After all, Hume denied that it was a truth at all. We need an explanation of the rationality of induction.

My own explanation is this. The sort of observational evidence which we have makes it rational to postulate *laws* which underly, and are in some sense distinct from, the observational evidence. The inference to the laws is a case of inference to the best explanation. (Whether this inference is governed by any rules of (non-deductive) logic is a matter about which I am agnostic.) If the inferred laws exist, then, of course, they entail conditional predictions about the unobserved ('if it is an F, then it will be a G').

Suppose, however, that laws of nature are conceived of as mere Humean uniformities. Then, I contend, this explanation of the necessity of the rationality of induction must fail. On that view, the law is nothing more than the conjunction of its observed manifestations with its unobserved manifestations. Such a law is not an explanation of the observations. Indeed, as Hume perceived, the true form of the inductive inference then becomes simply an inference from the observed cases to the unobserved cases. And, given that the law is just the observed plus the unobserved cases, *that* inference, I think Hume was right to argue, is an irrational inference.

Hume did not consider the possibility of using non-valid inductive arguments involving logical probabilities. But I contend that they are worthless where laws are conceived of as Hume conceived of them. Hume's instinct was right.

To tie up this argument it is necessary to ask why inference to the best explanation is rational. But that I think is analytic in a fairly obvious way. If making such an inference is not rational, what is? It may still be asked why the inference to underlying laws is the *best* explanation of our inductive evidence. The only answer to that is to challenge the questioner to find a better explanation.

I will now try to spell out the steps of this argument, concentrating upon the case against the Regularity theory.

1. *Inductive inference is rational.* We make inferences from the observed to the unobserved. Such inferences are central to the conduct of life. It is notorious among philosophers that these inferences are strictly invalid and also that they are very difficult to formalize. Are they nevertheless rational? In ordinary life we assume without question that they are rational. Hume, however, denied that they are rational. This constitutes his *inductive scepticism*.

Inductive scepticism is one of those sceptical theses that question part of the bed-rock of our beliefs. (As opposed, say, to scepticism about the existence of God, or the claims of psychical research.) It is this bed-rock of beliefs which G. E. Moore defended in his vindication of commonsense (1925). I think that he was right to defend them. This central core has the characteristic that we are much more certain of their truth than any of the philosophical arguments used to make us feel sceptical about them. We think, or we should think, that it is more likely that the arguments are unsound in some way (philosophy is very difficult) than that the beliefs are false.

One of the problems involved in casting doubt upon such beliefs is that the doubt-casting arguments require premisses, but it is not easy to see from where the premisses can be collected. To use premisses which are not drawn from the bed-rock of our beliefs is to bring the less certain as a reason for doubting the more certain. It appears that the best situation which the sceptic can hope for is to play off some of our truly fundamental beliefs against others. But such beliefs *seem* to cohere reasonably well. It takes a philosophically sophisticated argument to make a case for there being such an incoherence. But such an argument will again fall under suspicion for the reason already given: it will be less certain than our certainty that our system of fundamental beliefs is a coherent one.

It is to be noted also, as Hume so conspicuously noted, that a philosopher's denial of one of these fundamental beliefs always involves him in a certain amount of *mauvaise foi*. He may believe the sceptical theory, or, more likely, experience an illusion of belief, while he is in his study. But in his ordinary thinking and reasoning he will return to the unsceptical belief which he has officially repudiated. As Hume said:

Nature, by an absolute and uncontrollable necessity, has determined us to judge as well as to breathe and feel . . . (*Treatise*, Bk I, Pt IV, Sec. 1)

Now, of all our beliefs, the belief in the rationality of our inferences to the unobserved has claims to be our most basic belief of all. It is therefore a most serious philosophical objection to a philosophical theory if it has inductive scepticism as a consequence. But, I claim, the Regularity theory has just this consequence.

2. *That induction is rational is a necessary truth.* Some of our bed-rock beliefs are contingent ('I am now writing'), others are necessary ('7+5=12'). What is the status of our belief that inductive inference is rational? Is inductive scepticism contingently false or necessarily so? It seems that the rationality of inductive inference must be a necessary truth. For suppose it to be contingent. The question must surely come up then how we can know, or rationally believe, this contingent truth. It would seem to be the sort of contingent truth for which we would have to have inductive reasons. (How could we know it *a priori*?) But this involves a vicious regress of justification. Assuming then, as I am assuming, that we know or

54

rationally believe that inductive inference is rational, then it must be a necessary truth that induction is rational. (Earlier I failed to appreciate this point. David Stove convinced me of my error. He remains firm in his condemnation of all the further steps of my argument.)

3. *The explication of this necessary truth.* If it is a necessary truth, why is it a necessary truth? According to some philosophers, for instance Strawson (1952, Ch. 9), it is a necessary truth because it is part of the meaning of the word 'rational' that ordinary inductive inferences are rational. If necessary truths are analytic, then there is a sense in which this Strawsonian answer must be correct. It is nevertheless utterly unsatisfying. We want to be given some deeper reason why the rejecting of inductive inference as rational flies in the face of the meaning of the word 'rational'. (Compare this with somebody who said that 'no surface could be red and green all over at the same time' was guaranteed by the meanings of 'red' and 'green', but who told us nothing more.)

My object is to show that, if the Regularity theory of law is accepted, then we cannot explicate the necessity of the rationality of inductive inference. But it seems easiest to proceed by giving, at least in outline, my own explication of that necessity and then showing, by contrast, the difficulties involved in holding the Regularity view.

Suppose that all observed Fs are Gs, and that the further observational circumstances are such as to make it rational to believe that it is a law that Fs are Gs. Suppose that it is in fact a law. According to the Regularity view, the law is exhausted by the fact that the observed Fs are Gs and the unobserved Fs are Gs. I hold, however, that the law involves an extra thing, some further state of affairs. The presence of this extra thing (in my view a relation between universals, but I do not want to depend here upon the details of my view) serves, first, to explain why all the observed Fs are Gs, and, second, to entail that any unobserved Fs there are will be Gs.[3] The postulation of the extra thing is a case of inference to the best explanation. It is rational to postulate what best explains the phenomena. Induction is thus rational, because it is a case of inference to the best explanation.

All this is a promissory note, dependent upon a satisfactory theory of an extra thing which will serve both as best explainer of

[3] Subject to a qualifying condition which will emerge in Part II.

the observations and entailer of conclusions about the unobserved. I will try to redeem the note in Chapter 6, Section 7. But I hope enough has been said for the purpose of criticizing the Regularity theory. On my view, we have a pattern of inference which runs observed instances → law → unobserved instances. But the Regularity theorist cannot take such a pattern seriously. For him it reduces to: observed instances → observed instances + unobserved instances [his account of the law] → unobserved instances. Clearly this is no more than the pattern of inference: observed instances → unobserved instances. As a Regularity theorist, Hume understood this very well, and so constantly presented the inference in this way.

But if the inference is of this latter pattern, then it seems that Hume was also right to regard it as irrational. In the pattern of inference which I favour we have first a passage from observations to the entity which best explains the observations. It seems reasonable (!) to regard this as a rational, although non-deductive, inference. Second, we have a deductive passage from the entity to the unobserved cases. But what makes the Regularity theorist's preferred pattern of inference rational? On his view the law does not explain the observations. As Hume pointed out, the observed cases do not entail that the unobserved cases will resemble them. There seems to be no other way to explicate the rationality of the inference.

4. *Can the Regularity theorist's inference be saved by necessary connections in the world?* Hume maintains that there is no logically necessary connection between distinct existences, where present and future (or the observed and the unobserved) are taken to be paradigms of distinct existences. We can put his point in a contemporary way by saying that he denies that there is any *de re* logical necessity linking such distinct things as the present and the future. This is an essential step in his argument. If it could be successfully denied, then it might be possible to show the rationality of inductive inference while upholding a Regularity theory of the nature of laws.

I believe that Hume was right to deny the existence of a *de re* logical necessity linking the present and the future (the observed and the unobserved). But here I will confine myself to pointing out what a dialectically weak position the Regularity theorist will place himself in if he tries to introduce such a necessity. It is argued against the Regularity theory, for all the plausible reasons which we have already noted in previous chapters, that if it is a law of nature

56

that all Fs are Gs, then this is not a mere material implication. *Pace* the Regularity theory, some stronger connection, some necessity linking being F and being G, is required. This the Regularity theorist denies. But now suppose that the Regularity theorist, faced with difficulties about the Problem of Induction, tries to solve these difficulties by introducing *de re* necessary connections between present and future. Will not his denial of any nomic necessity over and above mere regularity become quite unprincipled?

5. *Can the Regularity theorist's inference be saved by non-deductive logic?* A second reaction to Hume's argument requires consideration. D. C. Williams (1947), D. C. Stove (1973) and J. L. Mackie (1979), Stove influenced by Williams, and Mackie by Stove, point out that Hume overlooked, and failed to argue against, the possibility that observational premises, while they do not *entail* any conclusion about the unobserved, may yet bestow some logical probability upon such conclusions. Consider the argument: 99% of Fs are Gs, *a* is an F, so, therefore, *a* is G. The premises do not entail the conclusion. Yet, given these premises, and given no other relevant information about *a*, it would obviously be rational to conclude that *a* is a G. So, it may be suggested, the evidence that all the observed Fs are Gs bestows some positive logical probability upon the proposition that unobserved Fs are also Gs.

A purely mathematical argument can be mounted. It is a necessary truth of arithmetic that a high proportion of large samples of a population match the distributions in the population itself. So, given a large number of observed Fs all of which are Gs, there is a high probability that the sample matches, or approximately matches, the population of all the Fs, unobserved as well as observed.

However, there is a conclusive reason for thinking that the principles of logical probability cannot, by themselves, solve the Regularity theorist's problem. The difficulty is that an argument from logical probability is of a purely formal sort. As a result, it cannot differentiate between more and less 'natural' classes. The fact that all hitherto observed emeralds are green might be taken to bestow a probability upon the hypothesis that all other emeralds are also green. But what of the hypothesis that all emeralds are green up to 2000 AD but blue thereafter? That is to say, what of the hypothesis that emeralds are grue? If the evidence we have now (before 2000 AD) bestows a certain logical probability on the hypothesis that all

57

emerals are green, why will it not bestow the same logical probability upon the hypothesis that all emeralds are grue?

Objection may be made to the predicate 'grue'. It may be said that
it involves essential reference to a particular time (2000 AD) which
'green' does not. It may be said that, on the 'grue' hypothesis, a
change occurs in emeralds at 2000 AD in a way that a change does not
occur on the 'green' hypothesis. To these objections Goodman has
given replies (1954). But we do not here need to consider whether
the replies are any good or not. For, if it is just a formal argument
from logical probability being advanced, any differences between
'green' and 'grue' must be irrelevant. The observed sample of
emeralds are green. The observed sample of emeralds are grue. The
mathematics is the same in both cases.

As a result, if an argument from logical probability is to assist the
Regularity theorist, he will have to use some more restricted principle. Obviously, he ought in some way to restrict the principle to
cases where natural predicates such as 'green' are used, as opposed to
unnatural predicates such as 'grue'. I would argue myself that this
involves bringing in universals. The observed Fs and the unobserved Fs must be genuinely *the same*, or at least objectively similar
where similarity is cashed in terms of universals. At any rate, let us
suppose that a restricted principle can be formulated, whether or not
it involves universals. The difficulty is that it remains impossible to
see how the new principle is to be justified.

To repeat. The Regularity theorist's problem is to justify an
inference from, say, observed emeralds to unobserved emeralds,
while denying that there is any intermediate law. For his concept of
law is that it is simply the greenness of observed emeralds plus the
greenness of unobserved emeralds. How then can it help him to add
the unobserved class to the observed class, and then argue from the
observed class to this total class using the mathematics of probability? His problem is to get from the observed class to a completely
disjoint class. No logical probability can help here. (And if it did, it
would equally help with unnatural as well as natural predicates.)

The argument as a whole may be put this way. The task is to
explicate the rationality of a inductive inference from P (say that all
observed emeralds are green) to R (say that unobserved emeralds are
green). I say that we can do this if we accept that P permits a non-
deductive inference to a *law* Q, that all emeralds are green, from
which it follows that R. But our concept of the law must be a

suitable one. If our concept of law is simply the concept of P+R, the inference pattern becomes P → (P+R), (P+R) → R, which reduces to P → R. *That* inference pattern Hume was right to think non-rational. It remains to show that there is a concept of Q, which allows rational P → Q. I believe that this demand can be satisfied if Q is conceived of as a relation between universals, and P → Q conceived of as a case of inference to the best explanation.

6. *Why is inference to the best explanation rational?* The inference from P to Q is not a deductive one. What then makes it rational? Only that Q, the existence of an appropriate law, is the best explanation which can be given of the observations. But why is an inference to the best explanation rational? Here I do think that we can finally appeal to the meanings of words, the appeal which Strawson and others made too soon. To infer to the best explanation is part of what it is to be rational. If that is not rational, what is?

It could still be wondered whether an appeal to laws is really the *best* explanation of P. To that we can reply with a challenge 'Produce a better, or equally good, explanation'. Perhaps the challenge can be met. We simply wait and see.

Notice finally that non-deductive logic may have a part to play in exhibiting the rationality of the inferences from P to Q. It may be that the inference to laws as the best explanations of the observed facts can be formalized, or partially formalized, and that principles of inductive logic have a part to play in the formalization. All I definitely deny is that such principles can aid the *Regularity* theorist to make a rational inference from the observed to the unobserved.

5

Can the Regularity theory be sophisticated?

1 PRELIMINARY

The strength of the case against the Naive Regularity theory of laws in particular, and the Regularity theory of laws in general, should now be evident. Some of the difficulties which have been rehearsed have been appreciated by Regularity theorists themselves. It is rather generally recognized that the class of Humean uniformities includes members which we do not wish to include among the laws of nature. A number of Regularity theorists have also recognized that it is not even easy to say what a uniformity is. The trouble here is provided by strange predicates such as 'grue'. Suppose that all Fs are Gs, but that the predicates 'F' and 'G' pick out what we would naturally think of as a heterogeneous miscellany. Is this a Humean uniformity? Intuitively, no. But the unsupplemented Naive Regularity theory seems to lack the resources to eliminate such 'uniformities'.

More recently, Regularity theorists have faced up to the difficulties posed for their view by the apparent existence in nature of irreducibly probabilistic laws. There is no simple emendation of the Naive theory available for dealing with such laws. For instance, it is no good substituting relative frequencies for uniformities, because certain relative frequencies are only *the most probable*, not the inevitable, manifestations of probabilistic laws. The only way to preserve a Regularity theory seems to be to introduce objective single-case chances or propensities, and then assert that probabilistic laws are uniformities linking more ordinary properties with these new sorts of property.

Against this background, let us consider various attempts to produce sophisticated versions of the Regularity theory. (For an account of the earlier literature, see Suchting, 1974.) The attempts fall under two heads in the first place. First, there are those who look for an *external* criterion to mark off 'good' from 'bad' uniformities.

60

The criterion given is always, in a broad sense, epistemic. It is a matter of our cognitive attitudes to the uniformities – what evidence we have for them, and so forth. Second, there are those who look for an *internal* criterion, something about the uniformities themselves. There are, in turn, two types of view here. First, there is Brian Skyrms' recent attempt (1980) to mark off the good uniformities as the *resilient* ones. This is an objectivist version of the Epistemic solution. Second, there is the Ramsey–Lewis view, where the criterion of goodness remains external to any individual uniformity, but it is internal to the whole class. Only those uniformities which hang together in a certain systematic way are accepted as laws of nature. In the rest of this chapter these three approaches will be criticized. This completes the case against the Regularity theory of laws.

2 EPISTEMIC RESTRICTION UPON UNIFORMITIES

Molnar (1969) gives the following account of such restrictions. What I have called the Naive Regularity theory requires to be supplemented by

a clause requiring *p* [the statement of Humean regularity] to be known in a certain way, or that the evidence for it be of a certain kind, or that the evidence be acquired in a certain manner. (p. 82)

Two quotations may help to give the flavour. Goodman says forth-rightly:

I want . . . to emphasize the Humean idea that rather than a sentence being used for prediction because it is a law, it is called a law because it is used for prediction . . . (1954, p. 26)

By contrast, there are laboured complexities from Ayer (quite foreign to his usual style!):

Accordingly I suggest that for someone to treat a statement of the form 'if anything has ϕ it has ψ' as expressing a law of nature, it is sufficient (i) that subject to a willingness to explain away exceptions he believes that in a non-trivial sense everything which in fact has ϕ has ψ (ii) that his belief that something which has ϕ has ψ is not liable to be weakened by the discovery that the object in question also has some other property X, provided (a) that X does not logically entail not$-\psi$ (b) that X is not a manifestation of not$-\phi$ (c) that the discovery that something had X would not in itself seriously weaken his belief that it had ϕ (d) that he does not regard the statement 'if anything has ϕ and not$-$X it has ψ' as a more exact statement of the generalization that he was intending to express. (1956, pp. 233–4)

61

Even all this is not supposed to give more than a sufficient condition for a law of nature! It is not necessary, partly because:

... clearly it makes sense to say that there are laws of nature which remain unknown. (p. 234)

Suchting (1974, pp. 76–7), besides referring to Goodman and Ayer, mentions Braithwaite (1927), Ramsey (1929) and Strawson (1952) among those who favour epistemic versions of the Regularity theory. Elements of such an approach are, of course, to be found in Hume himself. (See his second definition of 'cause' in the *Treatise*, Bk I, Pt III, Sec. XIV.) My criticism of Epistemic theories is indebted to Molnar, Suchting and Dretske (1977, pp. 254–5). Dretske gives further references.

The second quotation from Ayer gives the principal reason for rejecting any attempt to sophisticate the Regularity theory by adding epistemic conditions. A law can be unknown, its existence not even suspected. Hence a law cannot be a Humean uniformity to which persons have some epistemic attitude.

How might this objection be met? It is hard to see what the Epistemic theorist can do except appeal to counterfactuals. A Humean uniformity is a law if and only if either we have a certain epistemic attitude, A, to it, or, if certain other conditions C (presumably also epistemic conditions) had obtained, we would have had attitude A to it. For instance, suppose that H is a Humean uniformity of which in fact we know nothing. C might be coming to know (true) evidence E, and then, on the basis of this and ordinary scientific reasoning, coming to the rational belief that H obtained. Attitude A might be the attitude of using the proposition that H obtains both as a basis for predictions and in counterfactual reasoning.

An obvious analogy is the Phenomenalist's attempt to give the truth-conditions for statements about unobserved objects, events, *etc.* in terms of sense-experiences which perceivers would have if, contrary to fact, their circumstances were of a certain sort.

To mention the analogy is already to place the Epistemic theorist's appeal to counterfactuals under a cloud. The Phenomenalist's appeal to counterfactuals is known to face great difficulties. One serious problem for an Epistemic theorist is that his counterfactuals apparently demand the existence of certain laws: laws about epistemic attitudes. For what else would justify his counterfactuals?

But if so, his account is threatened by circularity. A Humean uniformity is a law if we would take a certain epistemic attitude, A, to it, under certain epistemic circumstances, C. Yet the conditional can only hold provided that there are laws suitably linking these epistemic attitudes with these circumstances. But what account is to be given of these laws?

The laws will have to be Humean uniformities. Furthermore, they must be uniformities to which we have the right epistemic attitudes.

It is not clear to me whether or not this account can avoid circularity. But, in any case, the following objection can be brought. It is clearly possible that there should be a universe governed by laws, and one in which there were some Humean uniformities which we would not wish to account laws, but in which there were no minds. (It might be very like our universe if, as seems likely enough, the emergence of rationality demands highly specific conditions.) But in this universe there would be no Humean regularities involving epistemic attitudes, and hence, according to the Epistemic theorist, no laws.

Could the Epistemic theorist who wishes to give an account of this law-governed but mindless universe, treat the required laws of epistemic attitude as *uninstantiated* laws? We have seen (Ch. 2, Sec. 7) that the concept of an uninstantiated law must be given some countenance. Functional laws, for instance, may involve 'missing values'. But what account can a Regularity theorist give of uninstantiated laws? For him, they must surely be in some way parasitic upon, perhaps deduced from, instantiated laws, that is, instantiated uniformities. But in a mindless universe, what would these regularities be? Even if there were certain actual regularities from which hypothetical regularities about the behaviour of minded objects could be extrapolated, this would be pure luck. It would depend upon the particular laws which happened to hold in the universe, for instance whether physicalism happened to be true. So any attempted escape *via* uninstantiated laws seems blocked.

In any case, Michael Tooley has pointed out to me a still more radical possibility which would rule out any appeal by the Epistemic theorist to counterfactuals based upon laws. Might there not have been laws of nature which actually rule out the possibility of there being any minds? For instance, the laws might have been such that they only permitted things of very simple structure to exist. Since the Epistemic theorist is a Regularity theorist he must hold that what the laws of nature are is a contingent matter. Hence he must allow the possibility of laws which make minds nomically impossible. But he can give no account of these in his terms.

Epistemic theories may also face another, more direct, threat of circularity. Can the required concepts of knowledge, rational belief, *etc.* be analysed without making appeal to the notion of law? Naturalistic accounts of these notions, at least, appeal to the notions of law and/or cause. (I have argued for an account of knowledge in terms of law in my 1973, Pt III.) Cause in turn *may* have to be analysed in terms of law.

There is a final, rather fundamental, difficulty for the Epistemic approach. Why is a certain Humean uniformity the object of the epistemic attitudes appropriate for laws, while another is not? If the reproach is to be avoided that the difference is ontologically arbitrary, then it must be said that the difference of attitude is based upon a real or supposed difference in the objective nature of the uniformities in question. (The epistemic counterfactuals associated with unknown laws will in particular require such an objective ground.) But if there are these objective differences, then why should not they *by themselves* serve to mark off the Humean uniformities which are to be accounted laws from those which are not to be so accounted? In this way, the Epistemic sophistication of the Regularity theory passes naturally over into either that of the Resiliency or the Systematic approach.

This last objection shows that an attempt to modify the Epistemic view by talking only about the regularities which it would be *rational* to treat in certain epistemic ways, must appeal to differences in the regularities which make rational the difference in epistemic attitude. The modification therefore passes over into one of the Objectivist or internal solutions although in a concealed manner.

3 THE RESILIENCY SOLUTION

Skyrms' view has already been discussed in Chapter 3, Section 5, in connection with probabilistic laws.[1] As a result, it can be dealt with fairly briefly here. Suppose it to be a Humean uniformity that Fs are

---

[1] It was noted there that Skyrms himself does not want to interpret resiliency in an objectivist way. But it is a natural and interesting way to take it.

Gs. What further condition will turn it into a law? We want Fs to be Gs *resiliently*, that is to say, we want there to be actual Fs which are Gs in every nomically possible circumstance. That demand, the demand for absolute resiliency, cannot be met, of course. But, Skyrms points out, we might get relative resiliency. It might be that there are Fs which are Hs, which are Js, which are Ks . . . where the class of factors {H,J,K . . .} covers a wide range of suitable circumstances. Then, and only then, the uniformity is a law.

How wide must the range of factors be, and what makes the factors suitable? Intuitively, it will be the instantiation of many factors which put Fs to the test, factors which would produce an F non-G if it is nomically possible to produce such a thing. Consider, for instance, Tooley's description of the case of Smith's garden (Ch. 3, Sec. 2):

All the fruit in Smith's garden at any time are apples. When one attempts to take an orange into the garden, it turns into an elephant. Bananas so treated become apples as they cross the boundary, while pears are resisted by a force that cannot be overcome. Cherry trees planted in the garden bear apples or they bear nothing at all. (1977, p. 686)

The generalization about the fruit in Smith's garden is highly resilient because it holds in a wide variety of circumstances *which could have been expected to falsify it if it was falsifiable.*

The objection, however, is obvious and has already been raised against Skyrms' treatment of probabilistic laws. Why should there not be laws which are in fact unresilient? If it is a law that Fs are Gs then, by definition, it is *potentially* resilient. It is not physically possible that there should be a K such that, if there is an F which is a K, it is not a G. But why should nature be so obliging as to furnish us with reasons for thinking that there is no such K? Why should there be Fs accompanied by factors which are plausible, but failed, candidates for being K? Why should not Smith's garden exist in a remote country which contained no fruit but apples, yet still it be a *law* that it bear nothing but apples? It seems to me that only a vulgar positivism could make us reject such a possibility.

For this reason, then, the Resiliency solution must be rejected. It is to be noted in any case that this solution to the problems faced by the Naive Regularity theory will have to incorporate many elements of the Systematic solution, still to be discussed. For how is the Resiliency theorist to give an account of what it is to be a factor which genuinely tests a putative law? He can only do this if he can filter out the nomically significant factors from others. It will be a matter, therefore, of his selecting among the Humean uniformities those which hang together to make a coherent system: the Systematic approach. Difficulties for the Systematic view will therefore, in general, be difficulties for the Resiliency approach.

4 SYSTEMATIC RESTRICTIONS UPON UNIFORMITIES

F. P. Ramsey put forward the Systematic view in a paper written in 1928, 'Universals of Law and of Fact' (Ramsey, 1978). He abandoned the view in a paper written in 1929, but there summarized it deftly, saying that the uniformities which we call laws are the

consequences of those propositions which we should take as axioms if we knew everything and organized it as simply as possible in a deductive system. (1978, p. 138)

This formulation makes the axioms laws because they are among the consequences of themselves.

A preliminary difficulty is that, on the face of it, Ramsey's suggestion is an epistemic one. As David Lewis says (1973, p. 73) it seems to involve 'a counterfactual about omniscience'. However, we may agree with Lewis (and Ramsey himself, 1978, pp. 131–2) that no such counterfactual is really involved. Consider the class of the Humean uniformities among which we select to form our deductive system. Even though many of the uniformities will be unknown, corresponding to each uniformity, known or unknown, is a true proposition. (It is clear that there are unknown truths. What they are is, fortunately, something which does not have to be discussed here.) It is an objective fact that certain deductive relations hold between these true propositions so that the propositions, and sub-sets of them, form various deductive systems. Standards of simplicity are perhaps human standards. But, it may be hoped, they are standards about which humans agree, and so the standards are in a sense objective.

Lewis endorses the Ramseyan view. He develops it thus:

Whatever we may or may not ever come to know, there exist (as abstract objects) innumerable true deductive systems: deductively closed, axiomatizable sets of true sentences. Of these true deductive systems, some can be axiomatized more *simply* than others. Also, some of them have more *strength*, or *information content*, than others. The virtues of simplicity and strength tend to conflict. Simplicity without strength can be had from pure logic, strength without simplicity from (the deductive closure of) an

66

almanac... What we value in a deductive system is a properly balanced combination of simplicity and strength – as much of both as truth and our way of balancing permit. (p. 73)

He goes on:

We can restate Ramsey's 1928 theory of lawhood as follows: a contingent generalization [a statement of Humean uniformity] is a *law of nature* if and only if it appears as a theorem (or axiom) in each of the true deductive systems that achieves a best combination of simplicity and strength. (p. 73)

It is to be noted that the class of Humean uniformities from which the laws of nature are to be selected can be thought of as including every 'vacuous' law. None of these laws bestow any strength. But inclusion of a selected few along with instantiated uniformities may increase the simplicity of systems of the latter by the filling in of gaps. These selected few are the uninstantiated laws recognized by scientists.

This Ramsey–Lewis suggestion seems to me to be the best that a Regularity theorist can do when faced with the problem of distinguishing between laws of nature and mere accidental Humean uniformities. It is certainly superior to Epistemic solutions of the problem. (It might be improved still further by incorporating elements of the Resiliency view.) Furthermore, as I will try to bring out at the end of this section, it is based upon a genuine insight. Nevertheless, it faces a number of difficulties. It is to be noted, also, that even if we grant that it solves the problem about accidental uniformities, it does little to meet the difficulties for a Regularity theory proposed in Chapters 3 and 4.

The *first* objection which may be made to the Systematic solution is that an element of subjectivism remains. We have already noticed that it has to involve our standards of simplicity, which, even granted that they are shared by all rational mankind, may not be shared by other rational creatures. The same point seems to hold for standards of strength. Lewis also refers to 'our way of balancing' simplicity and strength. May there not be irresoluble conflicts about the exact point of balance? A Rationalist temperament might value simplicity where an Empiricist valued strength. If such a conflict arose, there could for Lewis be no truth of the matter.[2]

---

[2] Lewis tells me that he thinks that the attraction of the Systematic view rests upon the (so far reasonable) hope that the winning system is so far ahead that it wins by *any* reasonable standards.

Second, the Systematic solution faces a difficulty involving Humean 'uniformities' picked out by predicates such as Goodman's 'grue'. If we take the best system formed from the natural, or non-grue-like, predicates, then it seems that, by introducing these strange predicates, systems which are just as good or even better might be formed.

Suppose, for instance, that the natural system contains three fundamental laws: Fs are Gs, Hs are Js, Ks are Ls. Let us unify them in the following way. Define an M as 'an F or an H or a K'. Define an N as 'a G, or a J or an L'. We then have a 'single' fundamental law: Ms are Ns. But now what is wrong with treating M-ness and N-ness as real properties linked by a real uniformity, and treating the original 'properties' as artificial divisions of the Ms and the Ns? M-ness and N-ness cannot be ruled out by an appeal to the criterion of simplicity. That criterion is applied to the deductive organization of sets of uniformities. It is only applied *after* sets of uniformities have already been formed.

Can it be said that, where the M–N 'law' has greater simplicity, it lacks the *strength* of the original generalizations? On the new system, given an F we can deduce that it is an N. But on the old system, we can deduce that it is a G, and G is a further specialization of N. However, this seems to beg the question. Suppose that the old system could have been improved, so that a theoretical identification of properties could have been made: $G = J = L$. To say that an F was a G would then have been no more informative than saying that it is a G or a J or an L. But the new predicate 'N' is being supposed to pick out a single property which the predicates 'G', 'J' and 'L' artificially break up. From the standpoint of the 'property' N, therefore, G is J, and J is L.

Goodman, and perhaps other Epistemic theorists, do not have to be overly concerned with this problem. For Goodman, the fact that we pick out certain regularities and project them onto the unobserved is what makes them laws. But this solution is unavailable to a Systematic theorist because of his much more Realistic view of laws.

However, I do not think that this is an insuperable difficulty for the Systematic theorist. What he must do, however, is to give *objective* criteria for distinguishing genuine from pseudo-uniformities. He cannot treat the classes of things linked together in uniformities as *mere* classes, or classes unified only by the application of the same (!) predicate to each member of the class. Instead, he will have to carve nature at the joints. He will have to appeal either to objective resemblances which hold together some, but only some, classes, or else to objective universals (properties, *etc.*) which are instantiated by some but only some classes. For myself, I believe that the Resemblance solution without universals breaks down. A Regularity theorist who wants to give objective criteria for real uniformities must be a Realist about universals.

In the *third* place, although I have already said that the Systematic view is open to the objections brought against the Regularity theory in Chapters 3 and 4, I would like to point in particular to the difficulty about counterfactuals. Epistemic theorists may be able to do something with this problem. For they can urge that it is our preparedness to extrapolate beyond actual instances falling under a uniformity to merely possible instances which, wholly or partly, *constitutes* the lawfulness of the uniformity. By comparison, what can the Systematic theorist say? Laws are those uniformities which form part of the best deductive systematization of the uniformities. If we imagine a new object and endow it with a certain property, or if we feign that a real object has a property which it actually lacks, what reason have we to think that its further properties will fit the general propositions of the best deductive system? The best deductive system is a mere *de facto* systematization. Why should new objects or changed objects conform to it?

Lewis suggests in reply to this difficulty that (a) the best deductive system of general propositions is an important feature of the world; and (b) counterfactuals hold important features fixed as far as possible. But importance is a relative matter. Suppose it to be a law that Fs are Gs, suppose that *a* is not F, but it is not an unreasonable suggestion that *a* be F. We say that if *a* had been an F, it would have been a G. According to Lewis we do this because the system in which the Humean uniformity that Fs are Gs fits, the system of laws so-called, is important to us. We therefore keep it constant even while supposing what we know to be false, that *a* is F. Suppose, however, that we, or our culture, were quite uninterested in the system of laws. Then, presumably, it would fail to be the case that if *a* were an F, then *a* would be a G.

But it does not seem that the truth-conditions for counterfactuals

69

can be as relative as that. We think that if *a* were an F, then *a* would *have* to be a G. Is this necessity only a necessity relative to standards of importance?

If the Systematic theorist is to give an objective account of such counterfactuals, his best chance seems to be Mackie's idea that it is a matter of inductive inference. But this depends, even waiving other difficulties, upon finding a solution of the Problem of Induction compatible with a Regularity theory of laws. I argued in Section 5 of the previous chapter that this cannot be done.

The *fourth* objection is that, like any coherence theory, the Systematic view yields the possibility of equally coherent, but incompatible, systematizations. In Chapter 3, Section 6, functional laws were discussed. Given variable magnitudes P and Q, it may be that only a finite number of these magnitudes (magnitude *types*) are instantiated omnitemporally. The instantiated magnitudes may be compatible with different, and incompatible, possible functional laws. In such a case, the Systematic view presumably takes 'the law' to be that expressed by the simplest formula, where both intrinsic simplicity, and simplicity of fit with other laws, are taken into account.

A conventionalist, subjectivist, tendency is already evident. But what of the case, already discussed, where there appear to be just three fundamental laws, all functional ones? L_1 and L_2 do not involve any uninstantiated values, are different in their mathematical nature, but are equally simple. The third law involves a choice between two formulae, 'L_3' and 'L_4', because it involves uninstantiated values. L_3 and L_4 would be equally simple, and L_3 closely resembles L_1, while L_4 closely resembles L_2. Either would appear to do equally well as the third law. It seems to be arbitrary which is said to be the law.

Lewis (1973, p. 73) said that something is a law of nature

if and only if it appears as a theorem (or axiom) in *each* of the true deductive systems that achieves a best combination of simplicity and strength. [my italics]

No doubt he did not say 'in *any* of the equally good true deductive systems', because, for example, this would make L_3 and L_4 both laws, and 'L_3' and 'L_4' would sustain incompatible counterfactuals. But Lewis' formulation means that, in the case which we have envisaged, there *is* no third law. This seems wrong also. I think the least evil is to say that an arbitrary decision has to be made as to whether L_3 or L_4 is the third law. The cost is the revelation that, in certain possible situations, the Ramsey–Lewis view yields no non-arbitrary answer.

Lewis might not be too worried by this difficulty. Perhaps such cases are part of what he has in mind when he says that lawhood 'has seemed a rather vague and difficult concept' (p. 73). Difficult it certainly is. But is it a vague one? Scrutinized through the spectacles of a Regularity theory, no doubt it is. But my own intuition is that the dividing line between laws and non-laws is a precise one. If the theory to be advanced in the second half of this book is anywhere near correct, then the dividing line is precise. And, comparing the theories, is not this difference in precision a disadvantage of the Systematic version of the Regularity theory?

I come finally to the *fifth* objection, which is the one on which I place by far the greatest weight. I begin by saying that I agree with Ramsey and Lewis that it seems that the uniformities which are manifestations of the laws of nature can be picked out from the whole class of Humean uniformities in the general way that they suggest. (Resiliency considerations may also be important.) But I deny that this is a necessary truth. I deny, what they assert, that their criterion is part of our concept of a law of nature.

Against them, I advance the following thesis. Consider the whole class of the Humean uniformities. Consider then *any* class formed by selecting members of this class, including the whole class and the null-class. I assert that it is logically possible that the uniformities in the selected class are manifestations of laws of nature, while the uniformities in the remainder class are mere accidental uniformities. It is logically possible that every Humean uniformity is the manifestation of a law of nature, that none are ('the Humean universe'), or that any other sub-class is the class of the manifestations of laws.[3]

How is this position to be argued for? An example already given in Chapter 2, Section 3, can be mentioned again. The following

---

[3] Suchting says: 'the actual number and distribution of instances of a universal [generalization] seem to be, with respect to that universal at least, a completely accidental matter which could not affect the law-likeness or otherwise of the universal' (1974, pp. 81–2). Suchting's point seems to be equally correct, and the reverse of the point just made. I am saying that one can keep the Humean uniformities fixed, and vary the laws indefinitely. He is saying that we can keep the laws fixed, and vary the number and distribution of their instances indefinitely. I am indebted to Michael Tooley for the observation that Suchting's and my points mirror each other in this way.

seems to be a meaningful supposition. Given the co-instantiation of a complex of physical properties, P,Q,R,S, it is a law that a further property, E, emerges. This emergent law might be quite unintegrated with the other laws of nature. It might be a 'nomological dangler'. Far from adding *simplicity* to the system of laws, the $(P,Q,R,S) \rightarrow E$ law would add complexity. Suppose further that the conjunction of P,Q,R and S is very rare in the history of the universe. The law will hardly add any *strength* to the system of laws. (Resiliency may also fail.) Indeed, the $(P,Q,R,S) \rightarrow E$ uniformity appears to be just the sort of uniformity that the Ramsey–Lewis theory of lawhood is designed to exclude. *Yet it might be a law*.

Here is another consideration. David Stove has pointed out (not in print) that although contemporary science with good reason views the laws of nature as forming an integrated system, this was not always so. In past centuries the working system of generalizations accepted was at least compatible with a much less integrated set of laws. It seemed quite likely then that laws of nature were such that the many different sorts of thing in the universe had each of them their irreducibly different ways of working.

Suppose that what then seemed likely enough to be the truth about the laws of nature had turned out in fact to be the case. The Systematic theorist can accept this possibility. He can say that, in that case, the true deductive system which achieves a best combination of simplicity and strength fails to achieve a very good combination of simplicity and strength. The winner is a winner out of a poor field.

But a difficulty remains. It is the integrated nature of the set of laws upon which the Systematic theorist relies to show that certain uniformities (the blackness of races of ravens, moas all dying before fifty) are mere accidents, and not laws. These uniformities do not fit into the simplest, strongest system. But if the simplest, strongest system is not very simple and strong, it is likely to lack the resources to eliminate such accidental uniformities from the privileged set. Let the accidental uniformity be no more than fairly widespread, and it must be admitted. The patricians, lacking organization among themselves, will lack the power to exclude pushy plebeians.

Yet might it not be a mere accident, not a law, that all races of ravens are black, that all moas die before fifty, and yet it be the case that the laws of our world cannot be given the degree of systematization necessary to exclude these uniformities?

For these reasons, then, I think that we ought to reject the Systematic sophistication of the Regularity theory. What remains to be explained is the undoubted appeal of the Systematic view. We will understand this appeal, I think, if we see that the postulation of laws is a case of inference to the best explanation. The thing to be explained is the observed regularity of the world. Now, other things being equal, of two systems of putative laws which are compatible with the observed regularities, the better explainer óf the regularities is the system which has the greater simplicity and strength. For the best explanation explains the most by means of the least. Explanation unifies.

But while this explains the appeal of the Systematic view, it does not justify it. There is *a* sense in which 'the best explanation' must be true, for if it is not true, it is not 'the best'. But what would be the best explanation if it were true, need not be true. It is logically possible that there are no laws at all, even though the regularities of the world are best explained by postulating systems of laws. Among such systems, those with the maximum strength and simplicity are, all other things being equal, to be preferred as explanations, although it is logically possible that the actual system of laws has less strength and simplicity than some other false systems.

If this is correct, then the Systematic approach mistakes good methodology about laws for analytic truth about lawhood.

So it seems that neither the Epistemic nor the Resiliency nor the Systematic approaches can bolster up the great weaknesses of the Regularity theory of laws. We seem well justified in looking for some other account of the nature of laws.

PART II

Laws of nature
as relations between universals

6

Laws of nature as relations between universals[1]

1 THE NEED FOR UNIVERSALS

It will be assumed from this point onwards that it is not possible to analyse:

(1) It is a law that Fs are Gs

as:

(2) All Fs are Gs.

Nor, it will be assumed, can the Regularity theorist improve upon (2) while still respecting the spirit of the Regularity theory of law.

It is natural, therefore, to consider whether (1) should be analysed as:

(3) It is physically necessary that Fs are Gs

or:

(4) It is logically necessary that Fs are Gs

where (3) is a contingent necessity, stronger than (2) but weaker than (4). My own preference is for (3) rather than (4), but I am not concerned to argue the point at present. But what I do want to argue in this section is that to countenance either (3) or (4), in a form which will mark any advance on (2), involves recognizing the reality of universals.

We are now saying that, for it to be a law that an F is a G, it must be *necessary* that an F is a G, in some sense of 'necessary'. But what is the basis in reality, the truth-maker, the ontological ground, of such necessity? I suggest that it can only be found in *what it is to be an F* and *what it is to be a G*.

[1] An earlier version of portions of this chapter appeared in *Philosophical Topics*, Vol. 13, No. 1, 1982.

In order to see the force of this contention, consider the class of Fs: a, b, c ... Fa necessitates Ga, Fb necessitates Gb ... and so on. Now consider the universal proposition: for all x, Fx necessitates Gx. Are we to suppose that this proposition is simply a way of bringing together all the individual necessitations? If we do suppose this, then we seem to have gone back to a form of the Regularity theory. The new version could meet the objection made to the orthodox Regularity theory that no inner necessity is provided for in the individual instantiations of the law. But it will be exposed to many of the other difficulties which we brought against the Regularity theory. For instance, no progress would have been made with the Problem of Induction. In the past, for all x, Fx necessitates Gx. But what good reason can we have to think that this pattern of necessitation will continue?

We need, then, to construe the law as something more than a mere collection of necessitations each holding in the individual case. How is this to be done? I do not see how it can be done unless it is agreed that there is something identical in each F which makes it an F, and something identical in each G which makes it a G. Then, and only then, can the collection of individual necessitations become more than a mere collection. For then, and only then, can we say that *being an F* necessitates *being a G* and, *because* of this, each individual F must be a G. But this is to say that the necessitation involved in a law of nature is a relation between universals.

Suppose that one is a Nominalist in the classical sense of the term, one who holds that everything there is is a particular, and a particular only. Because there is nothing identical in the different instantiations of the law, such a Nominalist, it seems, is forced to hold a Regularity theory of law. For if he attempts to hold any sort of necessitation theory, then he can point to no ontological ground for the necessity. He is nailed to Hume's cross. A Realist about universals may also hold a Regularity theory of law, and, indeed, will have great advantages over the Nominalist when it comes to saying what a *uniformity* is. But the Realist can also move beyond the Regularity theory. For he can hold that the uniformity is based upon something which is not a uniformity: a relationship holding between the universals involved in the uniformity.

It might be wondered whether even a relationship between universals can really advance beyond a mere uniformity. Suppose that the universal F is related to the universal G in such a way that Fs are

Gs. Might it not happen that at a certain point in time F and G come to be related in a different manner, so that it is no longer the case that Fs are Gs? If this possibility is admitted, it can hardly be denied that for *each* instantiation of F the relation between the two universals might be different. So the law that (all) Fs are Gs sinks to a mere uniformity again.

But to argue in this way is to fail to see what a relation between universals is like. If F and G are related by a dyadic relation, a relation whose terms are confined to these two universals, then it *cannot* be that they have this relation at one time or place, yet lack it at another. The universals F and G are exactly the same things at their different instantiations. They cannot dissolve into different F-nesses and G-nesses at different places and times: if they do, we are not dealing with unitary universals, that is, with universals. As a result, there can be no question of their being related in a certain way at one place and time, yet not being related in that way elsewhere. R(F,G) and ~R(F,G) are incompatible states of affairs. We have still to understand in concrete detail how such a relation is reflected at the level of particulars. But if it holds in one instance, then it holds in all, because it is the one identical thing in all the instances.

But, it may still be objected, the very same particular may have incompatible properties, including incompatible relational properties, at different times. Why, then, should not the universal F have R to G at one time, but have R to H, which is incompatible with G, or simply lack G, at another?

It is true that we speak of the same particular having incompatible properties at different times. But I take this to be an argument for saying that the true subjects of the incompatible properties are not identical. The true subjects are different temporal phases (parts) of the particular involved. The case where a thing is red all over today, and green all over tomorrow, is really little different from the case where it is today red at the top and green at the bottom. In the case of a universal, however, its instantiations at different times do not involve different parts of the universal. The identical universal is present in each instantiation.

It is possible to take the view that particulars, or at any rate selected particulars, 'true' particulars, do not have temporal parts. It is necessary then to introduce properties which involve a temporal index: *being red at* t_1, *being green at* t_2. Such properties are a particular case of what may be called 'quasi-universals'. The notion of a quasi-universal is one which will be discussed again in Section 7 of this chapter. They resemble universals in permitting a multitude of instances, but unlike universals proper they involve temporal or spatial restrictions.

Our present interest in quasi-universals is this. I have argued that if it is the case that N(F,G), that is if *being an F* necessitates *being a G*, then it must be the case that each F is a G.[2] But the following sceptical doubt may be raised. If a number of Fs have been observed during the interval t_1 to t_2, and during this time all are Gs, then this observation can be explained by postulating that N(F,G). *All* Fs will then be Gs. But why should we not also explain the phenomena by postulating instead a relation between F and the quasi-universal $G_{t_1 \rightarrow t_2}$?

I suppose that the answer to this, over and above any doubts which one may have about quasi-universals, is that explanatory principles should be as comprehensive and unifying as is compatible with what we know or believe. Given that all observed Fs are Gs, and given that the observations have been made between t_1 and t_2, then, other things being equal, the facts are better explained by the hypothesis that N(F,G) than by the hypothesis $N(F,G_{t_1 \rightarrow t_2})$.

Still another objection may be made. I have asserted that states of affairs such as N(F,G) are contingent. 'In a different possible world' it will not be the case that N(F,G). But now, it may be said, if we do not allow that the universal F can be related in a certain way to universal G at one time, and related in a different way to G at another time, why should we allow that the universals can be differently related in different worlds?

This, however, appears to be the original difficulty in a new form. If universals F and G are contingently related, then, by definition, they can be differently related in different worlds. But for them to be differently related at different times in the same world, different phases of the two universals would have to be present at the different times. But that supposition is not a real possibility, if it is universals that we are dealing with. Consider, by way of parallel, two point-instants in our world. Suppose it is a contingent fact that they are related by the relation R, a two-termed relation relating these point-instants. If they have that relation, it does not make sense to say that there was a time at which they gained it, or a time at

---

[2] This will have to be qualified. See Ch. 10, Sec. 4.

which they will lose it. They either have the relation or they lack it. At the same time, however, it remains *possible* that they should not have had that relation. The situation with N(F,G) is just the same.

Before leaving this section, I should call attention to one possibility which might be canvassed for moving beyond the Regularity theory of law, yet avoiding relations between universals. There are some Nominalists who accept the existence of objective relations of resemblance between particulars. They cannot analyse these resemblance relations in terms of common properties, because this would be to pass over into Realism, but they recognize relations of resemblance nevertheless. To have the property F is to be a member of a class of particulars which have certain resemblance relations to certain paradigm objects. Similarly for the property G. Such a Resemblance Nominalist may try saying that the ground of the necessity of an F being G is to be found in a relation between the network of resemblance relations which any F has to all the other Fs, and the network of resemblance relations which the same F has to all the other Gs (because it is a G).

I have criticized Resemblance Nominalism elsewhere (1978, Ch. 5), putting forward what are, for the most part, rather traditional, and I think decisive, difficulties. Even supposing that they can be surmounted, there is a further problem for the Resemblance Nominalist in the present situation. For him, there is still not strictly anything in common to each F, and to each G. This F resembles all the other Fs, but another F has its resemblance-relations to the members of a slightly different class. The same holds for the Gs. It is not clear that this shifting ground is sufficient to yield the required *unitary* connection between being an F and being a G. The Resemblance Nominalist would also face difficulties in the case of laws which have only one instantiation.

I think, therefore, that we can set aside solutions to the problem of nomic connection which try to use connections between networks of resemblance-relations. The only serious competitor to a Regularity view seems to be the view that a law is constituted by a relation between universals.

2 THE THEORY OF UNIVERSALS

Before going on to develop such a view, however, something requires to be said about the nature of universals. Even if Nominalism is rejected, different views of universals may be accepted.

These different views place constraints of differing severity upon theories of laws of nature as relations between universals. My own views on universals, developed in my 1978, place quite sharp restrictions upon the theory of laws. It may turn out that these restrictions are too sharp: the theory of laws is a vital proving-ground for the theory of universals. In the rest of this section, however, I will simply sketch, in fairly dogmatic fashion, the outlines of my theory of universals.

Universals I take to be monadic, that is, properties, or else dyadic, triadic ... *n*-adic, that is, relations. Universals are governed by a Principle of Instantiation. A property must be a property of some real particular; a relation must hold between real particulars. What is real, however, is not to be confined to the present. Past, present and future I take to be all and equally real. A universal need not be instantiated *now*.

A major reason for accepting the Principle of Instantiation is my desire to uphold, along with Realism about universals, the logically independent doctrine of Naturalism. Naturalism I define as the view that nothing else exists except the single, spatio-temporal, world, the world studied by physics, chemistry, cosmology and so on. (Whether Physicalism is true of this world, that is, whether this world can in principle be completely described using nothing but the concepts and laws of an ideal physics, is a further question. I do subscribe to Physicalism, but I regard it as more speculative than Naturalism.)

Those philosophers drawn to Naturalism are also regularly drawn to Nominalism. It seems natural to many to think of the spatio-temporal world as a world of mere particulars. And certainly if we admit *uninstantiated* universals we are abandoning the doctrine of Naturalism. But Naturalism combined with Nominalism has proved a very narrow ontological base. As a result, many philosophers drawn in these two directions have found themselves reluctantly forced to postulate extra entities: for instance, 'abstract' sets, and/or possible worlds. It is very worthy of remark, therefore, that, provided we restrict ourselves to *instantiated* universals, Naturalism can be combined with the rejection of Nominalism.[3] Given the Principle of Instantiation, universals can be brought into the spatio-temporal world, becoming simply the *repeatable* features of that world.

[3] As I learnt from my teacher, John Anderson.

The rejecting of uninstantiated universals involves one in rejecting the notion that a universal corresponds to every general
predicate. But I wish to reject this idea in any case. It may well be
that it is impossible to explain the use of general words without
postulating universals.[4] But we should not think that what universals there are are to be determined semantically, with universals
corresponding to each general word or phrase (or each possible
general word or phrase) which has a different meaning. I call this *a
priori* Realism (about universals). Against it, I wish to uphold an *a
posteriori* Realism. On the latter view, just what universals there are
in the world, that is, what (repeatable) properties particulars have,
and what (repeatable) relations hold between particulars, is to be
decided *a posteriori*, on the basis of total science.

A property, to take the simplest because monadic case, is something which is strictly *identical*, strictly the *same*, in all its different
instances. We should not assume that any old predicate, which in all
probability has come into existence for purely practical reasons,
applies in virtue of such identities. It is at least plausible that, as contemporary physics claims, the charge *e* on every electron is strictly
identical. It is very unlikely, as Wittgenstein perceived although he
was no Realist about universals, that all games have something identical which makes them all games.

I believe that this demand for strict identity across particulars
rules out disjunctive and negative universals, although my
argument involves some uncertainties. What are not ruled out,
however, are conjunctive and other structurally complex universals. Indeed, it seems to be an intelligible hypothesis, compatible
with everything that we know, that every universal is complex.
There may be no simple universals. (For detailed argument in
support of the above, see Armstrong, 1978, Ch. 14 and 15.) There is
also reason to rule out as pseudo-properties such things as the
identity of a thing with itself. The chief difficulty here is that
identity bestows no causal/nomic power.

Particulars are not to be reduced to bundles of universals, as
Russell and Blanshard argued, but nevertheless cannot exist
without properties. (The principle of the Rejection of Bare Particulars.) The mutual dependence of universals upon particulars, and
particulars upon universals, may be put by saying that neither can

---

[4] In my 1978, zeal for thrusting out semantics from the theory of universals led me to
shy away even from this obvious point. Michael Bradley (1979) rightly protested.

exist in independence of *states of affairs*. If a particular has a certain property, or two or more particulars are related, these are states of affairs. (Universals having properties, or being related, will also be states of affairs: higher-order states of affairs.) The bare particular and the pure universal are vicious abstractions from states of affairs. The particularity of a particular, and equally its properties and relations, are abstractions from states of affairs, but not vicious ones. The particularity of *a* is a non-vicious abstraction from all the states of affairs in which *a* figures. The property F (or F-ness) is a non-vicious abstraction from all the states of affairs where some particular has F (see Skyrms, 1981). The factors of particularity and universality are really there in states of affairs.

As is implied by the previous paragraph, in particular by talk about 'vicious abstraction', I take it to be of the essence of particularity and universality that they are found only in states of affairs. The Principle of Instantiation, and the Rejection of Bare Particulars, are, I think, necessary truths.

The question then arises whether properties and relations themselves fall under universals. Are there higher-order universals? Here again, in this very difficult field of enquiry, we must not proceed *a priori*, that is, semantically. We must not assign properties and relations to first-order properties and relations just because there is a predicate under which an indefinite number of those universals can be brought. Irreducibly higher-order universals, if they exist, must be postulated on an *a posteriori* basis.

Moving on to the more specific topic of higher-order *relations*, I am inclined to argue that the so-called 'internal' relations between universals, relations which appear to hold with logical necessity on the basis of the nature of the universals related, are not genuine relations. The 'relations' are not anything over and above the 'related' universals themselves. Many-place predicates are involved to which no relations correspond. My reasoning in support of this conclusion has an Irish flavour. If it can be shown *a priori* that two universals must stand in a certain relation, then there is no such relation for them to stand in. Nomic connection between universals, however, cannot be established *a priori*. It must be discovered *a posteriori*. So perhaps laws of nature can be treated as irreducibly second-order relations, genuine relations between universals. Indeed, I speculate that the laws of nature constitute the only irreducibly second-order relations between universals.

This sketch of a theory of universals will show some of the constraints which I think ought to be put upon an account of laws of nature as relations between universals.

3 A FIRST FORMULATION

During the 1970s, three philosophers, Fred Dretske, Michael Tooley and myself, all put forward the idea that the laws of nature are relations holding between universals. The idea is not a new one. It may be thought to have been anticipated by Plato (*Phaedo*, 102–107). But in Dretske (1977), Tooley (1977), and Armstrong (1978, Ch. 24), the idea seems to be more clearly articulated, and worked out in greater detail (especially in Tooley), than it had been in previous discussion. The utterly natural idea that the laws of nature link properties with properties had never entirely been lost sight of. But it was now made the object of some systematic attention.

Each of the three of us came to our view independently, and from different intellectual backgrounds. So it seems to be one of those not uncommon cases of an idea for which the time is ripe which is then hit upon independently by different people. It is true that Tooley and I met and talked over the topic at length before either of us published. But we had reached the central contention each by ourselves. We had even reached it by different routes. Tooley had been thinking about the laws of nature, and had decided that a satisfactory account of them could only be given if appeal were made to universals. I had been thinking about universals and then wondered whether laws might not be relations between these entities.

We all three had exactly the same idea. Suppose it to be a law that Fs are Gs. F-ness and G-ness are taken to be universals. A certain relation, a relation of non-logical or contingent necessitation, holds between F-ness and G-ness. This state of affairs may be symbolized as 'N(F,G)'. Although N(F,G) does not obtain of logical necessity, if it does obtain then it *entails* the corresponding Humean or cosmic uniformity: (x) $(Fx \supset Gx)$. That each F is a G, however, does not entail that F-ness has N to G-ness:

(1) $N(F,G) \rightarrow (x)$ $(Fx \supset Gx)$.
(2) (x) $(Fx \supset Gx) \nrightarrow N(F,G)$.

A scheme of this sort has attractive features. As already remarked, it is very natural to think of laws as linking properties. It seems natural to say that all Fs are Gs *because* being an F necessitates being a G. Again, one of the problems which plagues the Regularity theory, that of distinguishing between 'accidental' cosmic uniformities and those which are genuine manifestations of a law, is automatically solved. As will emerge, there are many other advantages.[5]

At the same time, however, the entailment in (1) is a very puzzling one. (I am indebted to a correspondence with David Lewis here.) Two universals are linked in a certain way. This state of affairs is in turn linked to a corresponding uniformity, where this second linkage is an entailment. Is the uniformity part of, actually contained in, the relation between the universals, so that the entailment has the form $(P\&Q) \to P$, with P = the uniformity? If so, the relation between the universals contains a surplus, Q, over and above the uniformity. What is this surplus, and how is it related to the uniformity? An alternative is that the entailment has the form $P \to (PvQ)$. This seems a bit more promising. But how is this form to be forced upon $N(F,G) \to (x) (Fx \supset Gx)$?[6]

If the entailment does not have one of these two simple formal structures, then it seems that we will have to say that the entailment holds in virtue of a *de re* necessity linking the relation between the universals, on the one hand, and the uniformity it 'produces', on the other. This is the picture which I get from the *Phaedo*. The Forms up in Heaven are related in a certain way, and, as a result, a uniformity is produced on earth. Such a doctrine is extremely mysterious. The mystery is only a little reduced by bringing the Forms to earth and letting them exist only in their instantiations. We still have the puzzle of a relation between the universals which logically necessitates something distinct from itself: the uniformity.

A closely connected difficulty is that the relation N which is said to hold between the universals lies under suspicion of being no more than 'that which ensures the corresponding uniformity'. Tooley

---

[5] Those who do not work in the Humean tradition of thought about law and cause may think that the entailment is too strong. They may think that the entailment holds only subject to the provision *that no interfering factor is present.*

  I am inclined to think that this qualification is correct. (See Ch. 10, Sec. 4, which discusses the distinction between 'iron' laws and 'oaken' laws.) But it will greatly simplify the discussion if the qualification can be ignored for the present.

[6] Of course '$N(F,G) \to (x) (Fx \supset Gx)$' can always be *tortured* into one of these two forms. But I am talking about formulations where 'P' and 'Q' stand for what it would be *natural* to take as elements in the situation.

explicitly says that it is a theoretical entity, introduced as that which explains the uniformity. But, of course, he thinks of this theoretical entity *realistically*. It has to have a nature of its own. Now what is this nature, and how does it ensure the uniformity?

Consider here that, *prima facie*, different laws involving the universals F and G are conceivable. It may be a law that Fs are Gs, or that no Fs are Gs (if we admit exclusion laws), or perhaps that, where something is an F, then something else is a G. It may therefore be asked how the relation between the universals determines the correct uniformity. Tooley introduces the formal device of a 'construction-function' which takes a given set of universals to the appropriate uniformities (1977, pp. 677–9). But how are we to understand the construction? Is it a real relationship in the world, holding between the universals and the uniformity? If so, the mystery is not dispelled, but rather increased. Now we have a relation between the universals, a construction-function and a uniformity. Or is it to be instrumentally conceived (which I am informed by Tooley was his intention)? If so, we are unhelpfully left once again with the related universals and the uniformity in which they issue.

I do not want to walk away from our formulae:

(1) $N(F,G) \rightarrow (x) (Fx \supset Gx)$
(2) $(x) (Fx \supset Gx) \nrightarrow N(F,G)$.

But it should be clear from this section that there is an urgent need to explain them.

It may be tempting, however, to deal with the problem as a logician might. Why not, while stipulating that F and G both be universals, do nothing more than place a modal operator of some sort in front of the statement of Humean uniformity? Why not analyse:

It is a law that Fs are Gs

as:

(1) $\boxed{c}$ $(x) (Fx \supset Gx)$

or even, if it is desired to deny the contingency of laws:

(2) $\Box$ $(x) (Fx \supset Gx)$?

The answer to this is not just that such a brisk procedure is merely a technical solution unaccompanied by metaphysical insight, although this objection is serious enough. It also faces an important internal difficulty. Because the fundamental connective involved is '⊃', defenders of these formulae must wrestle with the Paradoxes of Confirmation. For if this is what a law is, not only Fs which are Gs, but also non-Fs which are non-Gs, and non-Fs which are Gs, will confirm the existence of the nomic connection. We saw in Chapter 4, Section 3, that it may be possible to accept that non-Fs which are non-Gs in some degree confirm the hypothesis that it is a law that Fs are Gs. But what of non-Fs which are Gs? It seems that they do not confirm the law-hypothesis at all. This is a difficulty for the Regularity theory. The difficulty remains for an analysis of laws which simply places a modal operator in front of the Regularity formulae.

4 LAWS AS UNIVERSALS

Returning to our problem of understanding the entailment $N(F,G)$ → (x) $(Fx ⊃ Gx)$, the germ of a further elucidation was provided for me by Jim Lovelace, a graduate student at the University of Texas at Austin. He asked me whether the state of affairs $N(F,G)$, with which I wanted to identify the law that Fs are Gs, was itself a universal. Lovelace was not particularly pushing in that direction, he simply wanted to discover my view. But the more I considered the question, the more I began to see the attraction of taking $N(F,G)$ to be *both* the obtaining of a relation between universals, and a (complex) universal itself.

This idea, that the state of affairs constituted by $N(F,G)$ is itself a universal, will not solve the whole problem of understanding the entailment. In the end, as we shall see, the relation of nomic necessitation, N, will have to be accepted as a primitive. But if we can also accept that $N(F,G)$ is a universal, instantiated in the positive instances of the law, then, I think, it will be much easier to accept the primitive nature of N. It will be possible to see clearly that if N holds between F and G, then this involves a uniformity at the level of first-order particulars.

Just as Fa, or Rab, is a state of affairs (see Sec. 2), so $N(F,G)$ is a state of affairs. Rab is a state of affairs involving first-order particulars falling under a first-order universal. $N(F,G)$, by contrast, involves second-order particulars (first-order universals) falling under a second-order universal. The question is whether this state of affairs, $N(F,G)$, could simultaneously be a universal, a *first-order* universal?

If it could, then we might be on the way to understanding the relation between a law and the uniformity in which it manifests itself. We could understand this relation if we could understand the relation between a law and a particular instantiation of the law. For the Regularity theory the latter relation is perspicuous enough. It is the relation between a uniformity and a particular instance falling under the uniformity. But what is the relation between a law and a particular (positive) instantiation of the law, where the law is a relation between universals? If only we could think of this relation between universals as itself a (first-order) universal, then we could assimilate the relation between law and positive instantiation of the law to a particular case of that of a universal to its instances.

If the law is a universal, and its instantiations particulars of the universal, then, like any other universal, the law will be fully present in each instantiation. The relationship of universal to particular may involve problems. But they are problems which a believer in universals must face, and try to solve, in any case. What a gain if the way that a law stands to its positive instantiations could be assimilated to this relationship!

In my 1978, I said that a state of affairs such as $N(F,G)$ was not a universal, but a particular (Vol. I, p. 115, n. 1). I arrived at this view in the course of thinking about a very interesting phenomenon in the theory of universals which I called, rather melodramatically, 'the victory of particularity'. Consider particulars a, b and a universal R. The state of affairs, Rab, in which we may suppose them to be joined, is a particular, not a universal. For it is not susceptible of repetition in the way that a universal is. It is not a one which may run through a many. Particulars + universal = a particular. I then argued, as an afterthought, that $N(F,G)$ was equally insusceptible of repetition. Even universals + a higher-order universal = a (first-order) particular. States of affairs are always first-order particulars.

But perhaps the afterthought was a mistake. In the state of affairs, Rab, the *first-order particulars*, a and b, together with the *first-order universal*, R, yield a state of affairs which is a *first-order particular*. In the state of affairs, $N(F,G)$, the *second-order particulars*, F and G, together with the *second-order* universal, N, yield a state of affairs which, considerations of symmetry suggest, is a *second-order particular*. But a second-order particular is a first-order universal. Just the result which we want. N(F,G) would be a first-order universal, and its instances will be the positive instantiations of the law.

How is the suggestion to be worked out further? I propose that the state of affairs, the law, N(F,G), is a dyadic universal, that is, a relation, holding between states of affairs. Suppose that a particular object, a, is F, and so, because of the law N(F,G), it, a, is also G. This state of affairs, an instantiation of the law, has the form Rab, where R = N(F,G), a = a's being F, and b = a's being G:

(N(F,G)) (a's being F, a's being G).

Logicians are inclined to protest at this point. (Two logicians of my acquaintance have.) On the view being put forward, 'N(F,G)' can function as a complete statement, putting forward something which is true or false. At the same time, however, if N(F,G) is to be a universal, the 'N(F,G)' can also function as a mere part of a statement. Pavel Tichy (private communication) objects that N(F,G) cannot be both a dyadic attribute and an 0-adic attribute (his term for a state of affairs).

But I do not see why N(F,G) should not simultaneously be a (dyadic) universal and a state of affairs. Clearly it cannot simultaneously be a dyadic attribute and an '0-adic attribute' if these attributes are *of the same order*. But N(F,G) is being supposed to be a dyadic attribute *of the first order*, a first-order universal, while also being an '0-adic attribute' of the *second order*, i.e. a second-order state of affairs.

Suppose that one event – a change in something – precedes another event – say, a further change in the same thing. This whole complex is a state of affairs. In particular, it is a relation between two events. The related events – the two changes – are, however, themselves states of affairs. So we have a state of affairs of the form Rab, but where a and b are themselves states of affairs. Now if the particulars in a state of affairs can themselves be states of affairs, as in this case, why cannot universals also be states of affairs?

To continue the answer to Tichy, it seems clear that laws, although states of affairs, and real, are abstractions, that is, that they cannot exist in independence of other things. A universe could hardly consist of laws and nothing else. If laws are relations between universals, then the fact that laws are abstractions is explained, at any rate if it is granted that universals are abstractions, as, *contra* Plato, I take them to be. (I do not, of course, take them to be abstract in the Quinean/North American misuse of the term 'abstract'. In that misuse it is *Platonic* universals which are abstract!) For a relation between abstractions will itself be an abstraction.

Given, then, that relations between universals, i.e. laws, are abstractions, what sort of abstractions are they, and what are they abstractions from? We get a fairly clear answer to these questions if we say that laws are universals, and so are abstractions from particulars which instantiate those universals, i.e. abstractions from the particulars which instantiate (positively instantiate) the law. For a simple law like the law that Fs are Gs, the particulars instantiated by the law seem to be pairs of states of affairs: such things as a's being F, and a's being G.

At this point, however, a different and more sympathetic objection may be urged. Do we really need the complex formula:

(N(F,G)) (a's being F, a's being G)?

Could we not simply represent the instantiation of the law as:

N(a's being F, a's being G)?

The fact that the two states of affairs involve the two universals F and G, and these alone, might seem sufficient to ensure that the necessitation holds in virtue of the universals involved: that it is a relation of universals. (Whether the instantiation would then be an instance of N(F,G), i.e. whether N(F,G) would be a universal, is less clear.) However, although the matter is difficult, considerations to be advanced in the next section suggest that we do need to represent the situation in the more cumbrous way. I will drop the matter for the present.

Now we must face the problem, raised in the last section, that there may be different patterns of necessitation linking the very same universals. Perhaps it will be the case that a's being F necessitates, in virtue of the universals involved (F and G), that a is not a G (an exclusion law). Or perhaps a's being F necessitates that something else is G. Different relations of necessitation seem to be required. For the pattern of inference from 'a is F' is now different.

It is not clear whether we do require these other relations of necessitation. The matter will have to be explored later (Ch. 10, Sec. 6). But if we do, then we shall have to subscript 'N' to indicate the different patterns of necessitation which may hold between states of affairs. We will then have to think of N as a determinable relation of which N_1, N_2, ... etc. are determinate forms. The metaphysical status of determinables is a difficult issue, but perhaps that question can be evaded here.

However, it is the notion of necessitation itself, whether in determinable or determinate form, which produces the deepest protests and/or puzzlement. Perhaps the strain would be eased if it could be argued that this is the relation of logical necessitation. But I find it hard to bring myself to believe that the laws of nature are logical necessities, and will argue against this view in Chapter 11.

Consider mere conjunctions of universals. That is, consider the instantiated pattern of something being F, and also being G, where F and G are universals. This pattern may be thought of as itself a universal, having F and G as parts. Certainly, at least, the pattern is a *one* which can be instantiated in *many* particulars. But, given an F, it is not a compulsory pattern. There may be another instantiated pattern of something being F, and also being H, but where H is incompatible with G. The two patterns can be instantiated side by side (in different Fs).

Contrast this with the necessitation involved in laws. If a thing's being F necessitates that that thing is G, then, given that H and G are incompatible, it is not possible that a thing's being F also necessitates that thing being H. And so the following complaint may be made. At the end of all our explanations, this factor of necessitation remains unexplained.

This reproach is just, I think, but the inexplicability of necessitation just has to be accepted. Necessitation, the way that one Form (universal) brings another along with it as Plato puts it in the *Phaedo* (104d–105), is a primitive, or near primitive, which we are forced to postulate. Regularity theories of law reject it, but we have seen the inadequacy of Regularity theories. In rejecting Regularity theories we are committed to nomic *necessity* in some form or another. (It was perhaps a shortcoming of the original Dretske–Tooley–Armstrong formulation that this was not made evident.) We must admit it in the spirit of natural piety, to adopt Samuel Alexander's phrase.

Nevertheless, it may be possible to do a little more. The matter is speculative, but there does seem to be at least the logical possibility of a form of necessitation in nature which does not involve a relationship between universals. It may have a claim to be a still more primitive notion of necessitation. If so, it may provide an independent conceptual grip, an independent conceptual fix, upon the notion of necessitation. It may be that the notion of *necessitation between universals* can then be presented as the bringing together of antecedently understood, and conceptually independent, elements. In the next section this line of thought is developed.

5 CAUSATION AS A RELATION BETWEEN PARTICULARS

The story now to be told involves David Hume, Donald Davidson and Elizabeth Anscombe. It concerns causation.

Hume said that:

we may define a cause to be an object, followed by another, and where all the objects similar to the first are followed by objects similar to the second. (*Inquiry concerning Human Understanding*, Section VII)

As Davidson remarks (1967), Hume is here talking about *particular* causal sequences: this event causing that event. He is saying that to be such a sequence is to be an instance of a regular sequence. We might say that for a particular sequence to be causal is for it to fall under a law (conceived of as a regular sequence).

Hume's formulation strongly suggests, and has been taken by his followers to suggest, an epistemological point. To recognize a particular causal sequence *as causal* is to bring it under some sequence, or, as may be said, to bring it under some particular law.

When scrutinized, however, this epistemological point appears to be less than plausible. We are very often able to recognize that a certain singular sequence is a causal one, yet have absolutely no idea what regular sequence it could be an instance of, what law it could fall under. My favourite example here is one which I heard from Douglas Gasking. A small piece of stuff is observed to be dropped into a glass of liquid, in a laboratory, say. The next thing perceived to happen is that the glass explodes violently. Under these circumstances we would have little doubt that we had witnessed a particular causal sequence. The dropping of the stuff into the glass caused the explosion. But we might have absolutely no idea what was the regular sequence involved. We could not begin to formulate the law. Once alerted to the existence of such examples, we see that they are in fact ubiquitous.

Davidson is sympathetic to Hume's ontological position on causation. But faced with the epistemological difficulty he makes the

93

following suggestion. When we think that we have identified a particular sequence as causal, we do not necessarily claim to know any law governing the sequence, even in a quite rough and ready way. What we claim, rather, is that *there is* some description of the sequence in question under which the sequence is law-governed. We do not make a specific nomic claim, but an existential one. In this way, Davidson thinks, we can partially reconcile a Singularist theory of causation, such as that of C. J. Ducasse, with Hume's view:

The reconciliation ... depends on the distinction between knowing there is a law 'covering' two events and knowing what the law is: in my view, Ducasse is right that singular causal statements entail no law; Hume is right that they entail there is a law. (1967, p. 92 in Sosa)

Davidson's contention, however, really leaves him in a rather weak position *vis-à-vis* those who wish to uphold the possibility of singular causation *without* there being any law at all in the background, known or unknown. This is the point made by Miss Anscombe:

It is over and over again assumed that any singular causal proposition implies a universal statement running "Always when this, then that"; often assumed that true singular causal statements are derived from such 'inductively believed' universalities. Examples indeed are recalcitrant, but that does not seem to disturb. Even a philosopher acute enough to be conscious of this, such as Davidson, will say, without offering any reason at all for saying it, that a singular causal statement implies *that there is* such a true universal proposition – though perhaps we can never have knowledge of it. Such a thesis needs some reason for believing it! (1971, p. 81 in Sosa)

What is to be said about Miss Anscombe's contention? Suppose that one event causes another event. It is natural to think that both events have a great many characteristics which are causally irrelevant in this situation. If those characteristics had been absent, or had been altered in certain ways, the causal sequence would still have occurred. It may therefore be plausibly argued that there is an important sense in which the first event causes the second event only under certain descriptions. For those of us who are Realists about universals this will become the contention that what goes on here is one state of affairs (say, to give an oversimplified schema, a acquiring the property F) causing a second state of affairs (say, b acquiring the property G).

At this point we might think that Miss Anscombe's position is weak. If a's becoming F causes b to become G, and these are the causally relevant states of affairs, are we not in the presence of some F→G law?

However, I do not think that this conclusion really does follow. If a's becoming F causes b to become G, then there is an F→G law only if the first event causes the second event *in virtue of the universals F and G*. And while it is natural to expect the universals to be 'operative' in this way, I do not see how to prove that they must be so operative. For myself, I would think worse of the universe and these universals if they were not operative. Nevertheless, I think that Miss Anscombe can fairly claim that it is logically possible that a's becoming F should cause b to be G, where this causal connection is purely singular, simply a matter of *this* event causing *that* event. I think, therefore, that Miss Anscombe has the right of it against Davidson.

As just indicated, I do not much welcome the admission that purely singular causal connection is logically possible. I should like to believe that all causation is governed by law. Perhaps in fact it is. But I do not see how to exclude the logical possibility of causation without law. (In my 1978, I still accepted that cause logically must involve law. See Vol. II, p. 149.)

The importance for our argument of the notion of purely singular causation, causation without law, is that it brings out the logical possibility of *necessitation* without law. It brings out the possibility of one state of affairs, a's being F, say, necessitating a's being G, without any laws being involved. For reasons which will be developed later (Ch. 10, Sec. 7), we cannot identify causation with (natural) necessitation.[7] There are, or can be, cases of necessitation which are not cases of causation. As a result, we cannot identify causal laws with laws of nature, or purely singular causation with purely singular necessitation. But purely singular causation, if it occurs, is a *case* of purely singular necessitation, and, from the point of view of our present argument, it is the logical possibility of purely singular necessitation which is important.

The argument of this section is in fact linked to the point which came up in the previous section when we were wondering whether:

(1) $(N(F,G))$ (a's being F, a's being G)

---

[7] No positive theory of causation will be developed in this work.

could be simplified to:

(2) N(a's being F, a's being G).

The difficulty with (2), we can now see, is that it seems to be compatible with purely singular necessitation. The point may be brought out by saying that (2) is *compatible* with:

(3) N(b's being F, b's being H)

where a ≠ b and H is incompatible with G. (3), however, is *incompatible* with (1). So (2) is weaker than (1). Miss Anscombe's point about causation may be generalized by saying that a situation of the sort (2) is at least logically possible even though (1) is false.

A final remark on singular necessitation. A statement that one state of affairs necessitates another state of affairs must, it seems, still sustain counterfactuals even if the relation of necessitation is purely singular. Suppose that a's being F necessitates a's being G, but no law is involved. It can then be asserted that if a's being F had not obtained, and in the absence of other states of affairs necessitating a's being G, then a's being G might not have obtained. (The need for 'might' rather than 'would' is a response to an objection made to the 'would' formulation by Peter van Inwagen. He pointed out to me that the counterfactual has to allow for a's being G being an uncaused state of affairs and so occurring even though a's being F does not occur.)

6 NECESSITATION, UNIVERSALS AND LAWS

If the argument of the previous section has been correct, then it is now possible in some small degree further to elucidate the notion, central to our account of a law of nature, of one universal necessitating another. For we now have our 'independent fix' upon the notion of necessitation.

We may perhaps render 'N(F,G)', the assertion of a state of affairs which is simultaneously a relation, in words as follows:

Something's being F necessitates that same something's being G, in virtue of the universals F and G.

This is *not* to be taken simply as:

For all x, x being F necessitates that x is G.

because this would be to fall back, once again, into a form of the Regularity theory. Instead, as the phrase 'in virtue of the universals F and G' is supposed to indicate, what is involved is a real, irreducible, relation, a particular species of the necessitation relation, holding between the universals F and G (*being an F, being a G*). The related universals are abstractions from states of affairs, but not vicious abstractions, and their being related is itself an (abstract) state of affairs.

The concept of necessitation involved here is a relation holding between universals, between sorts of states of affairs, types rather than tokens. But, I suggest, it is essentially the same notion as the singular necessitation which, as we saw in the previous section, *might* hold between particular states of affairs, between tokens.

In this way, I hope, we finally obtain a reasonably perspicuous view of the entailment:

$$N(F,G) \rightarrow (x)\,(Fx \supset Gx).^8$$

Transfer in thought the concept of necessitation from the sphere of particular states of affairs, taken simply as particular, to the sphere of sorts or types of states of affairs, that is, universals. Instead of a's being F necessitating it to be the case that a is G, without benefit of law, we have instead something's being F necessitating that something to be G, where a type of state of affairs (the universal F) necessitates a type of state of affairs (the universal G). It is then clear that *if such a relation holds between the universals*, then it is automatic that *each* particular F determines that it is a G. *That is just the instantiation of the universal N(F,G) in particular cases.* The left-hand side of our formula represents the law, a state of affairs which is simultaneously a relation. The right-hand side of the formula represents the uniformity automatically resulting from the instantiation of this universal in its particulars.

So, in something of the spirit of John Locke's theory of complex ideas, we have put the concept of necessitation together with the concept of universals (types of states of affairs) to yield the notion of a law of nature.

---

[8] If we accept the view that there can be purely singular necessitations, then we can insert an intermediate term in the formula above:

$$N(F,G) \rightarrow (x)\,N(Fx,Gx) \rightarrow (x)\,(Fx \supset Gx).$$

None of the reverse entailments hold.

Objection may be made to this putting together. Even if the concept of particular necessitation is conceded to be a coherent concept, it may still be asked what is the justification for employing it in a new context: that of sorts of states of affairs, the realm of universals? I cannot prove that the transfer is justified. All I can do is to point to the explanatory value of the 'new complex idea' as a reason for thinking that it is a coherent concept. But I take it that inference to a good, with luck the best, explanation has force even in the sphere of metaphysical analysis.

It is worth noting that, in the new realm of universals, necessitation-statements still sustain counterfactuals. I am not referring to the ordinary counterfactuals sustained by law-statements, although we shall shortly see that the theory sketched does permit a plausible account of these in the way that the Regularity theory does not. I am thinking rather of counterfactuals parallel to those sustained by statements of purely singular necessitation. If a's being F determines a's being G, but purely as a matter of singular necessitation, then if a's being F had not obtained, and in the absence of other states of affairs necessitating a's being G, then a's being G might not have obtained. Similarly, if being an F did not exist (states of affairs of the *being an F* sort did not exist) then, in the absence of other factors which would have necessitated the instantiation (existence) of G, G might not have been instantiated (might not have existed).

Before finishing this section, let us note that the introduction of necessitation between singular states of affairs leads to an intuitively quite satisfying picture. We have the possibility of necessity at every level. At the first level we have nothing more than a first-order state of affairs necessitating a further first-order state of affairs, for example:

$$N(a\text{'s being F}, a\text{'s being G}).$$

At the second level, we have a first-order universal, a *type* of first-order states of affairs, necessitating a further first-order universal, again a *type* of first-order states of affairs, for example:

$$(N(F,G)) (a\text{'s being F}, a\text{'s being G}).$$

With this necessitation between *universals* we have what are called laws of nature. At a third level, we would have a second-order universal, that is, a universal instantiated by first-order universals, a *type* of second-order states of affairs, necessitating a further second-order universal, also a *type* of second-order states of affairs. This would be a second-order law, a law about first-order laws. There is no *a priori* limit to this ascending series.

There is no difficulty in treating N, the first-order relation holding between particular states of affairs, as the same thing as the second-order relation N found in N(F,G), and the third-order relation N found in second-order laws. There is no particular reason to accept a Principle of Order Invariance: that if a universal is of order M in one instantiation, then it is of order M in all instantiations. (See my 1978, Ch. 23, Sec. II.)

7 ADVANTAGES AND SOME DISADVANTAGES OF CONCEIVING OF LAWS OF NATURE AS RELATIONS BETWEEN UNIVERSALS

I hope that I have now provided at least the outlines of a coherent version of the view that the laws of nature are relations between universals. In this section I will consider in turn all the difficulties which I previously brought against the Regularity theory, and examine the fortunes of the new theory in the face of these difficulties.

In the *first* place, it is clear that the problem of accidental Humean uniformities is no problem for the present view. The single-case Humean uniformities, the Humean uniformities correlated with local uniformities and the uniformities which are only uniformities because certain possibilities are not realized, need not be taken as manifestations of laws. For no appropriate relation may hold between the universals involved. Being a moa need not necessitate dying before fifty.

In the *second* place, pseudo-uniformities expressed by means of predicates such as 'grue' likewise present no problem. For it is plausible to say, on the basis of total science, that 'grue' is a predicate to which no genuine, that is, unitary, universal corresponds. Where there are no universals, there is no relation between universals.

In the *third* place, we saw that a Regularity theory of laws has some difficulty with the phenomenon of uninstantiated laws. The Naive Regularity view must either bar all possible laws of this sort, or none of them. But in fact we want to take a more selective attitude, admitting as true a few, but rejecting as false most, statements of uninstantiated law. It may be that a sophisticated

99

Regularity theory, in particular the Systematic view, can admit uninstantiated laws in this selective way, as statements which make a contribution to 'rounding out' the system of instantiated uniformities.

If laws of nature are relations between universals, and themselves universals, and if uninstantiated universals are rejected, as I am inclined to think that they should be, then it seems that uninstantiated laws will have to be rejected. Yet, as just noted, we want to admit some.

In the next chapter it will be argued that some statements of uninstantiated law can be accepted because they are concealed counterfactuals, saying not what laws hold, but what laws *would* hold in certain unrealized conditions.

In the *fourth* place, spatio-temporally limited laws ('laws of cosmic epochs') which it seems that the Regularity theory could be stretched to admit, must be ruled out if laws of nature are relations between universals. It may be argued that this is a plus for the Regularity theory. But this possible plus is quite overshadowed by the problem created for the Regularity theory by *small-scale* regularities. Tooley's case, the case of Smith's garden which will bear nothing but apples, seems to be completely incompatible with a Regularity view.

But what of the view that laws of nature are relations between universals? Is it not also refuted by Smith's garden? I do not think it is, but it is true that it must be modified in some degree. What seems required is that we introduce the notion of a *quasi-universal*. An example of such an entity would be *fruit grown in Smith's garden*. This is not a universal, because it involves essential reference to a particular: Smith's garden. But it is not quite a particular either, because it is capable of repetition. In fact it would answer to Aristotle's condition for a universal, because it is 'predicable of many'. Normally, we would simply think of this as a particular part of the extension of a universal. But if it turns out to be required for a law, then we take it more seriously as an entity in its own right, a quasi-universal which can be related in the usual way to the universal of *being an apple*. We have N (an F having R to a certain garden, A).[9]

---

[9] The Smith's garden case now appears as an *intermediate case* between fully general laws of nature, involving relations between universals, and the purely particular necessitations between states of affairs envisaged by Miss Anscombe. A purely particular necessitation is the limiting case of a law such as the law governing Smith's

If this is a possible modification of the relations between universals theory, then it can be applied back to the problem of laws which are restricted to cosmic epochs. They too would be laws which relate a certain range of quasi-universals (Fs in epoch 13, say) to universals, by a necessitation relation.

So the Universals theory can make shift to deal with the problem posed by the Smith's garden case. If the shift succeeds, then it also works for laws restricted to cosmic epochs. The Regularity theory, on the other hand, although it can make a shift to deal with the problem of cosmic epochs, seems helpless before the Smith's garden case.

In the *fifth* place, the Universals theory can give an elegant account of the nature of infinitely qualified laws, at any rate if negative universals are rejected. I will leave discussion of this until Chapter 10, Section 4.

In the *sixth* place, we saw that the Regularity theory faces great difficulty in accounting for irreducibly probabilistic laws. It seems necessary to introduce objective single-case propensities or chances, something which runs very much against the spirit, at least, of the Regularity theory. In Chapter 9, I will consider how an account of laws of nature as relations between universals could handle probabilistic laws. The view which I favour involves a *probability of necessitation in the particular case*, but holding in virtue of a relation of the universals involved.

In the *seventh* place, we saw that functional laws with missing values create some embarrassment for the Regularity theory. For different functional formulae may all fit the actually instantiated values. A Naive Regularity theory will have to take *all* the formulae to express laws. A more sophisticated theory has nothing but considerations of simplicity and coherence to determine which of the formulae is to count as *the* real law.

Although the Universals theory does encounter some problems with functional laws (the subject of the next chapter), it need have no truck with the quasi-conventionalism adumbrated in the previous sentence. As will be shown, there can be objective relations between universals which will determine what functional

garden. But because the limiting case is purely singular, we would not call it a *law*. If objective single-case propensities, with propensity less than 1, are allowed to be logically possible, then we must admit singular probabilifications as well as singular necessitations.

formula expresses the real law. Functional laws turn out to be higher-order laws.

In the *eighth* place, we saw that the Regularity theory of law is unable to provide an inner connection for the individual instantiations of the law. The necessity which obtains when *a*'s being F necessitates *a*'s being G is purely external. It is *constituted* by the fact that all the other Fs (if any) are Gs. The demand for an inner necessity is triumphantly met by a Universals theory. The problem is solved in a peculiarly satisfactory way if the law is itself conceived of as a universal, and the instantiations of the law as instances falling under that universal. For then the law is fully present in each instance.

In the *ninth* place, if all the observed Fs are Gs, then it seems to be an explanation of this fact that it is a law that Fs are Gs. But, given the Regularity theory, the explanatory element seems to vanish. For to say that all the observed Fs are Gs because all the Fs are Gs involves explaining the observations in terms of themselves. Suppose, however, that the law, if it exists, is the holding of an irreducible relationship of necessitation between the universals F and G. To postulate such a necessitation *unifies* the given phenomenon (which is a mark of explanation), and leads to further predictions extending beyond what is observed.

In the *tenth* place, the Regularity theory is exposed to at least one of the Paradoxes of Confirmation. Observing an F which is a G confirms that it is a law that Fs are Gs. It is possible to argue that a non-G non-F confirms the law. But it seems clear that non-Fs which are Gs in no way confirm the law. Yet, given the Regularity theory of law, where the statement of the law becomes a universally quantified statement of material implication, non-Fs which are Gs would confirm the law.

The confirmation which an F which is a G gives to the hypothesis that it is a law that Fs are Gs is no puzzle for the Universals theory. If the law holds, then the observation is *explained*. So the observation confirms the existence of the law. A puzzle arises, however, about non-G non-Fs. At the intuitive level, it is rather unclear whether they have confirmatory value. Certain arguments to show that they do confirm the law seem to fail (Ch. 4, Sec. 3). However, there is one argument for saying that non-G non-Fs confirm which appears to have force. If it is a law that Fs are Gs, then this does seem to explain concerning non-Gs why they are all non-Fs. Hence a non-G

102

non-F may be thought to confirm the law. At the same time, however, non-G non-Fs do not seem to have the same confirmatory value as FGs.

As already mentioned in Chapter 4, I believe it can be made plausible that non-G non-Fs are *second-grade* confirmers of the law. Notice first that the fact that it is a law that Fs are Gs does nothing to explain the existence of non-Gs. (It ensures the existence of Fs.) But *if* there are non-Gs, then each of them must be a non-F. The class of non-Gs, therefore, is a class whose members put the law-hypothesis to the test. The non-Gs must be either Fs or non-Fs. If they are Fs, it is not a law that Fs are Gs. Non-G *non-Fs*, therefore, represent failures to falsify within a class of instances where there is a logical possibility of falsification. This seems to be confirmation of a sort, although it is not the direct confirmation given by Fs which are Gs. Fs which are Gs also yield this second-grade confirmation, but in addition they confirm directly.

In the *eleventh* place, the Regularity theory is not able, while the Universals theory is able, to explain why statements of law sustain counterfactuals. Suppose it to be a law that Fs are Gs, but that *a* is not F. In general, at least, we will be prepared to conclude that if *a* were an F, it would be a G. Suppose, however, that laws are mere Humean uniformities. We are then in thought adding a new member to the class of Fs. There seems to be no particular reason why the new member should maintain the uniformity. Suppose, however, that the law is constituted by the fact that something's being F necessitates that something being G, a connection holding in virtue of the universals involved. If we now add *a* to the class of Fs we will, in general, have every reason to think that the F→G necessity is maintained. To suppose a new red thing does not change the nature of redness. To suppose a new F does not change the nature of the universal F. So why should not N(F,G) obtain in the imagined state of affairs?

In the *twelfth* place the Regularity theory involves inductive scepticism. Given the Regularity conception of a law of nature, inductive inference cannot be rational. Suppose that the observed Fs are all Gs, and that Fs have been observed in a wide variety of conditions. What good, if non-valid, argument is there to the conclusion that unobserved Fs are Gs? Unobserved Fs will be Gs only if it is a law that Fs are Gs. But if the law is simply the conjunction of the observed and the unobserved cases, no appeal to the law can have any value. The inference will be a straight inference from the observed to the unobserved. But then, it was argued, there is no way to show that the inference is rational.

I believe that the Universals theory can do better. The postulation of a connection between universals can provide an explanation of an observed regularity in a way that postulating a Humean uniformity cannot. The inference to a connection of universals is a case of an inference to the best explanation. A series of states of affairs is observed, each a case of an F being a G. No Fs which are not Gs are observed. The postulation of the single state of affairs, the law $N(F,G)$, gives a unified account of what is otherwise a mere series. Furthermore, it deductively yields a prediction which enables it to be tested, the prediction that all other Fs will be Gs. It is therefore a good explanation of the phenomena. With luck, it is the best. It may well be, of course, that, although a regularity is observed, we think it unlikely that the terms 'F' and 'G' pick out genuine universals. The inference then may be of a less concrete sort. We might infer, for instance, that some boundary condition C obtains, that there exist universals $F^\star$ and $G^\star$, that it is a law that $F^\star$s under conditions C are all $G^\star$s, that this connection suffices to ensure that all Fs in C are Gs, but yet not know what C, $F^\star$ and $G^\star$ actually are. But an inference to some such underlying pattern might still be the best explanation of the uniformity.

If this is correct, then induction becomes a particular case of the inference to explanatory ('theoretical') entities. The law, a relation between universals, is a theoretical entity, postulation of which explains the observed phenomena and predicts further observations. Many philosophers of science have distinguished between 'simple induction' – the argument from observed Fs to all Fs – and the argument to hidden or theoretical entities (Peirce's 'abduction'). It seems to be a great and intellectually encouraging simplification that, given our account of laws, the two sorts of argument are shown to be not really two.

Can inferences to laws be formalized, or partially formalized? In particular, can a non-deductive logic of inductive inference be developed? The matter lies beyond the sphere of my competence, but the idea seems quite promising. Tooley suggests (1977, p. 693):

if relations among universals are truth-makers for laws, the truth-maker for a given law is, in a sense, an "atomic" fact, and it would seem perfectly justified, given standard principles of confirmation theory, to assign some non-zero probability to this fact's obtaining.

This is an initial probability, or logical probability on a tautology. I am sceptical of the possibility of making any interesting assignments of such probabilities. (Should not Empiricists be suspicious of them?)[10] But if all the observed Fs have been G, then it certainly seems reasonable to assign a positive probability on that evidence to the hypothesis that it is a law that Fs are Gs.

What handles remain for the inductive sceptic? It seems that he might raise two doubts. He might ask what reason there is to think that laws construed as irreducible relations between universals constitute the *best* explanation of the observed regularity of the world. More fundamentally, he might ask what reason there is to think that the observed regularities of the world have any explanation at all.

There do seem to be other possible explanations of the regularity of the world. Perhaps, as Berkeley thought, the regularities in things reflect no power in the things themselves, but only a particular determination of the will of God to have ordinary things ('ideas' for Berkeley) behave in a regular manner. If it seemed best to him, he could abrogate the so-called 'laws of nature' tomorrow.

The answer to doubts such as these is simply to admit them. There can be no guarantee that the explanatory scheme which we favour is in fact the best explanatory scheme. All that can be done is to spell out all proposed schemes as fully as possible, and try to see which scheme fits the apparent facts best. We avail ourselves in this enterprise of whatever apparently good cannons of explanation we possess or can develop. The basic insight here seems to be involved in the concept of a good explanation: that it should genuinely unify, and that it should be genuinely informative.

A more thoroughly sceptical approach will ask what reason we have to think that the regularities of the world have any explanation at all. Might not the world be a Humean world, mimicking a world governed by genuine laws? Or, even if there are necessitations, might they not all be purely singular? If, as I would grant, these are logical possibilities, why should we move beyond these possibilities?

But if it be granted, as I think it should be granted, that laws, if they exist, would constitute a good, probably the best, explanation of the regularities of the world, then I do not think that the sceptic's

---

[10] Peter Forrest points out another difficulty for Tooley here. Given, what seems correct, that there are an infinite number of *possible* universals, will not the initial probability assignable to a given law be infinitesimal only? Such infinitesimal assignments will do nothing to further the justification of induction.

position is very strong. A good explanation of the phenomena is, presumably, a rational explanation of the phenomena. It is surely a great advance in the battle against the sceptic to be able to say 'This is a, perhaps the, rational explanation of the phenomena, although it is logically possible that the phenomena have no rational explanation.' After all, a burden of Hume's complaint against inductive reasoning is that it is not rational. Inferring to the best explanation is not a deductive process, but it is rational. And laws as relations between universals do explain observed regularities, and explain them well, although laws as mere uniformities do not explain observed regularities at all.

We may also ask the inductive sceptic what reason he has to believe that there are any observed regularities to explain. It is logically possible that our world is a Humean world. Solipsism of the present moment is also logically possible, as the sceptic well knows. If there is no good reason to move beyond the regularities of the world to laws which are more than regularities, then there is equally no good reason for him to move beyond his present observations and/or sensations to a regular world.

In the *thirteenth*, and final, place, I add a new point. The Universals theory allows us to understand, and to sympathize with, the notion that laws of nature *govern* particular states of affairs. Because of the imperfect analogy between social law and law of nature, it is clear that there must be an element of metaphor in this notion. But if the Regularity theory is correct then the metaphor is totally misleading, a mere product of metaphysical confusion embedded in ordinary speech and thought. But if laws of nature are relations between universals (and are universals), then the laws do have a relative independence from the states which instantiate them. This explains the bite of the metaphor.

At a later point (Ch. 10, Sec. 4), a distinction will be drawn between 'iron' and 'oaken' laws. Unlike iron laws, oaken laws do not hold *no matter what*. They hold only in the absence of interfering factors, and such an absence is not a further factor. A law of nature of this sort has an even closer, if still imperfect, resemblance to social law. For there is an (admittedly weak) sense in which it can 'fail to apply' or even 'be broken'.

Before leaving this topic, and although this chapter is already far too long, we do need to look at an argument used by Braithwaite and others with the object of showing that, because the Regularity account of laws claims *less* than other 'stronger' accounts, the latter accounts will be exposed not to less, but to more sceptical doubt. This will be the matter for a final section.

To sum up this section. It seems that in the areas where the Regularity theory of law conspicuously fails, the Universals theory for the most part conspicuously succeeds. Of course, this is not the end of the matter. There remains always the question of other bulges in the carpet. The Universals theory can smooth out the bulges which the Regularity theory creates. But perhaps in doing so the Universals theory creates worse bulges of its own elsewhere.

This is what we must now investigate. We shall see that the Universals theory involves some real problems and uncertainties. My judgement is that these problems and uncertainties are not of the overwhelming sort which the Regularity theory faces. Perhaps, however, this is a matter for others rather than myself to decide. At any rate, I think that enough has been said in its defence, and enough against its main opponent, to show that a theory of laws as relations between universals is well worth investigating.

8 BRAITHWAITE'S AND POPPER'S ARGUMENT

In his book *Scientific Explanation* (1968, first edn. 1953), Richard Braithwaite puts forward the following argument:

Another reason for starting with the constant-conjunction view is that, according to it, scientific laws are logically weaker propositions than they would be on any alternative view of their nature. On any other view, a scientific law, while including a generalization, states something more than the generalization. Thus the assumption that a scientific law states nothing beyond a generalization is the most modest assumption that can be made. This modesty is of great importance in considering the problem of induction. It is difficult enough to justify our belief in scientific laws when they are regarded simply as generalizations; the task becomes more difficult if we are required to justify belief in propositions which are more than generalizations. This fact does not seem to me to have been sufficiently recognized by many of those who criticize the constant-conjunction view for affording no sound basis for induction. (1968, pp. 11–12)

The same argument is used, although in a hypothetical manner, by Karl Popper in his *Logic of Scientific Discovery* (1959, Appendix):

To a student of method who opposes the doctrine of induction and adheres to the theory of falsification, there is not much difference between the view that laws are nothing but strictly universal statements and the view that they are 'necessary': in both cases, we can only test our conjecture by attempted refutations.

To the inductivist there is a crucial difference here: he ought to reject the idea of 'necessary' laws, since these, being logically stronger, must be even less accessible to induction than mere universal statements. (p. 437)

The argument reappears, more cautiously put, in D. H. Mellor (1980):

The debatable question is whether laws are more than generalizations, and if so, what more. Now if giving laws one content rather than another made the problem of induction soluble for them, this would be a strong argument for giving them that content. But since I believe no such solution is presently available for any credible content, I must look to other arguments. Hume's problem [the problem of induction] does, however, provide a reason for preferring weak readings of natural laws. The less a law says, the less there is to be certified in claiming it to be true. (p. 108)

To restate the argument. Suppose that we have good inductive evidence, E, for its being a law that Fs are Gs. The Regularity theorist interprets the law as being constituted by the fact that all Fs are Gs. I have argued that the law is a necessitation relation holding between the universals F and G: N(F,G). I assert, however, that N(F,G) entails that all Fs are Gs, and I deny the reverse entailment. So 'N(F,G)' is logically stronger than 'all Fs are Gs'. Hence it should be *harder* to establish N(F,G) on the basis of E than it is to establish that all Fs are Gs.

The first point to be made about this argument may be illustrated by considering the dispute between Instrumentalism and Realism with regard to scientific theories. Rather loosely following Van Fraassen (1980, p. 36) we may compare the instrumentalist to the atheist. He denies that there are any scientific entities lying beyond the observable ones. The Realist is like the theist. He asserts the existence of scientific entities lying beyond the observable ones. Both may be said to be 'dogmatists'. Both assert propositions which go beyond the observed. The Instrumentalist asserts that nothing lies beyond the observed. The Realist asserts that theoretical entities lie beyond, and explain, the observed. The proposition which sticks to the observational evidence is the 'agnostic' view which neither denies nor asserts the existence of theoretical entities Realistically conceived. (This is the view which Van Fraassen recommends as reasonable.)

Suppose, then, that we have good inductive evidence for believing that it is a law that Fs are Gs. What sort of thing should we take the law to be? The 'atheistical' view is that it is the fact that each F is G, and nothing else. The 'theistic' view is that it is a relationship between universals which entails, without being entailed by, the fact that each F is G. The 'agnostic' view is that the law is *at least* the fact that each F is G, and that it may or may not be something more.

Now it is clear that not only the 'theistic' but also the 'atheistic' view of laws is logically stronger than the 'agnostic' view. It is the agnostic view, therefore, which the Braithwaite–Popper argument should favour. (I am indebted to Michael Tooley for pointing out to me the analogy with Van Fraassen's argument.)

It may be said that the 'agnostic' view of the law, involving as it does a disjunction and an exclusive one at that, is not a view in which we can remain. Suppose this to be so. Have we then got any reason to come down on the 'atheistical' rather than the 'theistic' side of the disjunction? The principles of logical probability, which are the principles appealed to in this argument, give us no reason. These principles make no distinction between negative and positive propositions, between the absence of a relationship of universals and its presence. From the standpoint of the principles of logical probability, 'atheist' and 'theist' are equally dogmatic.

Of course, the 'atheist', the Regularity theorist, does seem to be asserting something weaker than the 'theist', the upholder of the Universals theory. But it is clear wherein that weakness lies. Unlike the principles of logical probability, *Occam's Razor* does distinguish between lacks and absences, on the one hand, and the corresponding presences of entities, on the other. It favours lacks and absences and disfavours presences.

It seems, then, that the real drive behind the Braithwaite–Popper argument is not really a point about logical content at all, but that it rests upon a covert appeal to Occam's Razor. The Razor, however, says that entities are not to be multiplied *beyond necessity*. The first five chapters in this work may therefore be tendered in evidence to show that the postulation of mere regularities is inadequate as an account of what it is to be a law that Fs are Gs.

A second difficulty for the argument is that, at best, it could only be used to support the *Naive* Regularity theory of laws. A sophisticated Regularity theory, whether in an Epistemic or Resiliency or Systematic version, does not hold that 'It is a law that Fs are Gs' can be translated as 'All Fs are Gs'. It is necessary that all Fs are Gs, but something further must be added: some epistemic, or, preferably, some resiliency or systematic conditions. Hence, simply considering logical probabilities, the formal situation for a sophisticated Regularity theory is the same as that for the Universals theory. So if the argument is a good one, it gives us not only a reason for preferring a Regularity theory to the Universals theory, but also a reason for preferring the Naive Regularity theory to a sophisticated Regularity theory.

But, I hope, if the first five chapters of this work have done anything, they have shown the utter untenability of the Naive Regularity theory. It must be abandoned. The Braithwaite–Popper argument then gives us no guidance as to whether it should be abandoned for a sophisticated Regularity theory, or some other theory.

It seems clear, therefore, that there is no particular reason to take heed of the argument. If there are positive reasons to prefer the Universals theory over the Regularity theory, then the argument in no way weakens those reasons. I have argued, of course, that there are such reasons.

7

Functional laws

It turns out that the problem of giving an account of functional laws is very closely bound up with the problem of uninstantiated laws. I will approach the problem of functional laws *via* an account of 'missing values' of such laws.

We will consider a functional law of the simplest sort. Let P and Q be distinct variable magnitudes,[1] and f be some functional constant. Let the law be manifested in the uniformity:

$$(x)\ (P)\ (Px \supset (\exists Q)\ (Qx\ \&\ Q = f(P))).$$

Here 'P' and 'Q' are restricted variables ranging over possible values (values which are properties) of the distinct magnitudes P and Q. The function is a total function, that is to say, there is a value of Q associated with each value of P. (This last requirement is made only to simplify the discussion.) Now consider the individual values of the variable 'P'. For each of these values, which are perhaps indenumerable in number, we can state a law, a law with a very simple form. Suppose that P_1 is such an individual value, and suppose that the value of $f(P_1)$ happens to be Q_1. We then have good old $N(P_1Q_1)$, manifesting itself in:

$$(x)\ (P_1x \supset Q_1x).$$

This suggests a *preliminary* way of thinking about the functional law. We can think of it as a conjunction (perhaps an infinite conjunction) of a set of simple laws each having the form just displayed: it is a law that P_Ns are Q_Ns.

Suppose now that P involves a missing member of the family.

---

[1] These magnitudes are to be thought of as families of properties. *Cf.* Swoyer (1982, p. 205): 'many philosophers think of laws as involving physical magnitudes rather than properties, often explicating such magnitudes as functions from sets of physical objects into the real numbers, and for such purposes as axiomatisation this can be useful. Nevertheless a function like "rest mass in kilograms" will map an
• object to 5.3 *because* of something about the object, *viz.* the mass that it has, rather than conversely.'

Property P_0 is omnitemporally never instantiated. $f(P_0)$, however, yields a determinate value: property Q_0. We therefore assert it to be a law that P_0s are Q_0s. We have $N(P_0, Q_0)$, 'manifesting' itself in (x) $(P_0 x \supset Q_0 x)$. But the question arises what is the justification for asserting this uninstantiated law. Why are we justified in adding it to the set of instantiated laws involving P and Q?

A Regularity theory can only solve the problem in a semi-conventionalist manner. It gives us the simplest system to assume that the missing value of Q will be f of P_0. A Universals theory, if it is in addition prepared to admit (omnitemporally) uninstantiated universals, can solve the problem in a completely Realistic way. The universal, P_0, can exist, although uninstantiated, the universal, Q_0, can also exist, even if uninstantiated, and P_0 and Q_0 could be related by the appropriate higher-order relation. Observation of *instantiated* values will then constitute the evidence for believing that in fact all this is the case.

We, however, while admitting universals, wish to admit only instantiated universals. Universals are abstractions from states of affairs. They are, indeed, sorts or types of states of affairs. What is such a view to say about the uninstantiated $P_0 \rightarrow Q_0$ law?

The view which I wish to put forward is that a statement of uninstantiated law should be construed as a counterfactual. Instances of the universal P_0 do not exist, that is, P_0 does not exist. Hence the $P_0 \rightarrow Q_0$ law does not exist. But if there were P_0s, that is, if P_0 existed, then P_0s would be governed by the law that P_0s are all Q_0s. Statements of uninstantiated law are really only statements about what laws would hold if, contrary to fact, certain universals were instantiated, that is, existed. I thus admit uninstantiated laws, but only as logically secondary cases of laws.

To continue to work this idea out. We are for the moment thinking of the functional law as a conjunction (perhaps infinite) of laws each having the simple form: it is a law that P_Ns are Q_Ns. But by what right do we extrapolate (counterfactually) from this bunch of laws to the 'law' that P_0s are Q_0s? The problem must remind us of the more ordinary problem of extrapolating from the actual set of Fs, each of which is a G, to the conclusion that, if particular a were an F, as it is not, then a would be a G. In the latter case, the counterfactual will be sustained if it is a *law* that Fs are Gs. Laws, we are further assuming, are relations between actually instantiated universals. So it seems that what is required in order to license our extrapolation to

112

the $P_0{\rightarrow}Q_0$ 'law' is that there be a law governing the conjunction of laws of the $P_N{\rightarrow}Q_N$ sort. The statement of this law, in conjunction with the counterfactual supposition that P_0 exists, will yield the $P_0{\rightarrow}Q_0$ law. The law governing the conjunction of laws must then be construed, given our programme, as a relation between actually instantiated universals.

We thus reach the conception of a functional law as a higher-order law which governs, indeed in this particular case completely determines the nature of, a set of lower-order laws. If there were no such higher-order law, but instead a mere coincidental conjunction, perhaps infinite, of first-order laws, then there would be no justification for making statements of uninstantiated law. Furthermore, if we reduce the higher-order law to a mere regularity, it will no more sustain counterfactuals than will a first-order law construed as a mere regularity.

Pursuing this idea, how are we to render our (especially simple) functional law linking the variable magnitudes P and Q? It will have this form. It is a law [second-order] concerning P-type properties, that, if a particular [first-order] has one of these properties, then it is a law [first-order] both that this particular has a Q-type property, and that a certain relation [the function: $Q=f(P)$] holds between this P-type and this Q-type property.[2]

We are developing the conception of laws of nature as relations between universals, states of affairs which are simultaneously universals. It is therefore required that the notion of a P-type property and a Q-type property be each the notion of a universal. The universals must each be *ones*, running through the *many* constituted by the P-type properties, and the Q-type properties, respectively. They will therefore have to be higher-order universals, properties of properties. It is here that certain problems arise, problems which we will need to consider shortly.

But first let us think about the form of the law. Can it be represented simply as N(P,Q), with N a third-order universal, P and Q second-order universals, and the second-order state of affairs N(P,Q) also a second-order universal? In fact, the formula 'N(P,Q)'

---

[2] It is to be noted that it would be possible for a second-order law of this sort *itself* to be an uninstantiated law. But, if our account of uninstantiated laws is correct, it would then be necessary at some point to reach a still higher-order law which is an *instantiated* law. From this the uninstantiated second-order 'law' could be counterfactually derived.

is a little too simple. What we have rather is N (being a P-type property, being a Q-type property such that Q is a function, f, of that same P-type property). It can be shortened to N(P, a Q such that $Q = f(P)$). This second-order state of affairs will also be a second-order dyadic universal (Ch. 6, Sec. 4), and its instances will be pairs of first-order universals of which the first member is an instance of P and the second member is the appropriate instance of Q. The instances of the law will thus be first-order laws of nature. The account is parallel to that given of N(F,G), but with everything moved up one order.

Since N is the same relation as that to be found in N(F,G), then, from the second-order law as it was formulated in the previous paragraph, first-order laws can be deduced. For example, it can be deduced that something's having the property P_1 necessitates that that same thing has Q_1, where $Q_1 = f(P_1)$. In this case, the second-order law not only governs the first-order law, but fully determines its content. But it is possible to have second-order laws which govern first-order laws without fully determining the latter's content. We will meet hypothetical examples in the next chapter.

But the real problem here seems to be raised by the required second-order universals, P and Q. A typical class of P-type or Q-type properties would be the class of the determinate masses. Can it be said that the determinate mass-properties (such as the property of being one kilogram exact) all have the common property of *being a mass*? P and Q ought to be common properties of this sort. Now, while the *predicate* 'being a mass' certainly applies to all and only this class of properties, it is less clear that we are entitled to say that *being a mass* is a genuine property of determinate masses.

Being a mass is a determinable, and the individual mass-universals are determinates falling under that determinable. In Part VI of my 1978 (Vol. II) I argued that there are no determinable universals, only determinates. A particular class of determinates is a class of universals having a certain ordered structure. (I suggested that this structure was governed by 'relations' of partial identity holding between the universals involved.) But I argued that there is no element genuinely common to each universal in the class in virtue of which it is a member of that class. The argument is difficult, and I am less than fully confident of it, but there is some reason to be suspicious of such properties as *being a mass*.

We have seen that the state of affairs N(F,G) is simultaneously a first-order relation. If *being a mass* is a property of properties, then *one kilogram's being a mass* will be a second-order state of affairs, $M(K)$, and this state of affairs, by symmetry, will also be a first-order property which will attach to first-order particulars, such as this balance-weight. This may seem unnecessary reduplication. Why need the balance-weight have *both* the property K and the property $M(K)$? And if it has $M(K)$, will it not have $M_1(K)$, $M_2(K)$ ... where M_1, M_2 ... are determinates intermediate between M and K? (As redness is between colour and fully determinate shade.) Realists about properties should be careful about properties! They should not multiply them in the reckless way favoured by those for whom properties are the mere shadows of predicates or are constituted by classes of particulars.

But perhaps this difficulty can be answered. Properties are to be postulated on an *a posteriori* basis. In particular, they are to be postulated because and where natural science demands them. Now, if there are functional laws linking being some mass with some other determinable property, then we have a need to postulate a *property* of being a mass, a common nature possessed by the determinate mass-universals. We do not need the intermediate determinables. So perhaps determinable universals can be admitted on a *selective* basis.

If this justification for such second-order properties fails, there remain a couple of positions which might be tried. In my 1978 discussion (Ch. 24, Sec. 3) I canvassed the possibility of moving away from determinables to still more general properties, and in particular to the formal nature of the ordered structure possessed by the classes of determinates in question. We could imagine a higher-order law which linked *all* those classes of determinate properties which have the same formal structure with further classes of determinate properties, the latter classes all having the same or another formal structure, according to some formula.

The difficulty about this is that nature might not be so obliging. Perhaps the class of P-type properties is linked with the class of Q-type properties according to a certain formula, but the class of R-type properties, a class with exactly the same formal structure as the class of P-type properties, is linked to the class of S-type properties in a quite different manner. The P→Q and the R→S connections might require *distinct* higher-order laws.

A somewhat shoddy third solution is that what we have here is a higher-order equivalent of 'cosmic epochs'. Laws of cosmic epochs restrict the scope of laws to particular temporal epochs (or spatial areas). We have grudgingly admitted the possibility of such laws (Ch. 3, Sec. 1). If they exist, they involve a necessitation relation, holding not between universal and universal, but between a quasi-universal (*F in a certain epoch*) and a universal. Think now of all the universals that there are as forming a 'space'. A class of determinates is a class of adjoining universals taking up a certain 'area' of this space. It can then be suggested that the higher-order law is restricted in its scope to this area of universals. Different laws hold in different areas. It would be a matter of *second-order* quasi-universals.

This survey of suggestions for uniting the classes of universals linked in functional laws indicates that the conception of functional laws as higher-order laws is not without its problems. But something of the sort seems required if we are to give an account of *uninstantiated* functional laws within the scope of a Universals theory, yet not countenance uninstantiated universals. The most hopeful line seems to argue for higher-order universals corresponding to *some* determinable properties *viz.* those required for functional laws.

116

8

Uninstantiated laws

In the previous chapter an account of uninstantiated laws was given. According to this view, strictly there are no uninstantiated laws. Statements of uninstantiated law tell us that a certain law would govern the antecedent universal, if, contrary to fact, that universal existed, that is, was somewhere instantiated. Such an account deals fairly easily with the problem of 'missing values' of functional laws. But certain cases of uninstantiated laws have been suggested by Michael Tooley (1977) which the counterfactual account appears to be unable to handle.

1 TOOLEY'S CASES

The cases to be discussed are not actual uninstantiated laws proposed by scientists. They are imaginary situations where, it is plausible to say, we should be inclined to postulate uninstantiated laws. Tooley himself was not concerned with the topic of uninstantiated laws for its own sake. Rather he wanted to use the cases, first to criticize the Regularity theory, and second to support the view that laws of nature are relations between universals. I largely followed him in his estimation of the cases in my 1978 (Ch. 24). Now I have doubts.

The Fundamental Particle case (1977, p. 669). Tooley imagines a world containing ten, and only ten, types of fundamental particle. Allowing that a particle may interact with a particle of its own type as well as with particles of other types, this allows for 55 interaction laws governing the interaction of pairs of particles. Suppose that 54 of these laws are known. They prove in each case to be so idiosyncratic that, given *any* 53 of them, the nature of the 54th could not be known, or even rationally conjectured, antecedently to experience. But suppose that the 55th law, the law of the interaction of B-type with J-type particles, is not known. This occurs because, although

117

this type of interaction is physically possible, yet boundary conditions in the universe are such that, throughout all time, no B-particle is ever close enough to a J-particle to interact with it.

Tooley claims that, in this situation, we would have good reason to assert the existence of an uninstantiated law governing B–J interactions. But although we would have good reason to assert the existence of the law, we would not be able even to conjecture what its detailed content was. This is quite different from the case of the missing values of functional laws. In the latter cases, we can say just how the uninstantiated particulars would behave, if they were instantiated.

The Emergent property case (1977, p. 685). I will present the case in my own way. Suppose that there are, as it seems that there perfectly well might be, irreducible, simple, emergent properties. (On certain views of the secondary qualities, they will be of this nature.) Suppose that there is a sequence of complex structural properties, P,Q,R..., which form a scale of some sort. Suppose that the conjunction of P,Q and R, when instantiated by a particular, gives rise to the simple emergent property E. Suppose that the conjunction of Q,R and S gives rise to the distinct simple emergent property F, and R,S and T to G. Under circumstances of this sort, we might have good reason to believe that S,T and U, when conjoined, would give rise to yet another simple emergent property. Suppose, however, that, although the conjunction of S,T and U is physically possible, in fact it is never at any time instantiated. Would we not have good reason to believe that an uninstantiated law linked the conjunction of S,T and U with some further simple emergent property?

This Emergent property case resembles the Fundamental particle case. We would have good reason to believe that a law existed, but would be unable to specify its full content. We could specify the antecedent circumstances of the law (if S,T,U...) together with the general nature, but not the specific content, of the consequent.

2 TOOLEY'S CONCLUSIONS

Tooley draws three conclusions from his cases. Two are agreeable, but the third is not.

The first conclusion is that the Regularity theory is false. The Regularity theory can give no account of uninstantiated laws of the sort which, if Tooley is correct, his cases force us to postulate. In the case of uninstantiated laws governing 'missing values' of functional laws, the Regularity theory, if in some difficulties, is not helpless. It is at least colourable that the uninstantiated laws are asserted because they fill up gaps in the system of instantiated uniformities, that is, instantiated laws. But if we agree that, in Tooley's cases, definite and determinate uninstantiated laws exist, but yet that this determinate content is unknown to us, no account at all of these laws is available to a Regularity theorist.

Second, Tooley draws the conclusion that laws of nature must be relations between universals. For what could act as truth-maker or ontological ground for these uninstantiated laws except the universals involved and their relations? In the Fundamental particle case, for instance, there must be a relation between those universals which make a B-type particle a particle of the B-type, and the universals which make a J-type particle a particle of the J-type. The existence and nature of the other 54 laws gives us good reason to postulate such a relation, but at the same time keeps us in the dark as to the exact nature of the relation.

So far, very promising. The Regularity theory has been humbled, the Universals theory exalted. But, as Tooley points out, there is bitter to swallow with the sweet. For, third, it appears that these uninstantiated laws require uninstantiated universals. Consider the B–J law. It has the form 'If a B-type particle and a J-type particle have the relation R, then...' Now the complex universal, the whole state of affairs of a B having R to a J, which constitutes the antecedent universal, is, by hypothesis, never instantiated. Yet it is this universal which requires to be related to the consequent universal (which perhaps is never instantiated either). So it seems that Tooley's cases force us to admit at least the logical possibility of uninstantiated universals.

Can the difficulty be escaped? Can we not give an account of such 'laws' by appealing to counterfactuals about what laws would hold if the antecedent universals were instantiated? May we not say that if the B–R–J universal existed, as it does not, then there would be a (necessitating or probabilifying) relation holding between it and some further universal? What would be the truth-makers for this counterfactual? Well, there do exist B-type particles, and J-type particles. Furthermore, the relation R is, presumably, elsewhere instantiated. The unknown consequent universal may be uninstantiated. But surely at least the constituent universals of the

119

consequent universal will be instantiated? So there will exist a class of universals to act as truth-makers.

I put forward this solution in my 1978 (Vol. II, p. 156–7). But, alas, this Tooley-without-tears solution founders on the Emergent property case. There the uninstantiated law has the form: if S,T,U, then an unknown simple property emerges. It is an intelligible supposition that the conjunction of S,T and U (all separately instantiated, it may be supposed) is a *necessary* condition for the emergence of the simple property. If so, since the conjunction S,T, and U is uninstantiated at any time, the simple property is uninstantiated at any time. Since the property is simple, it can have no instantiated constituents. So the truth-maker for the uninstantiated S,T,U law includes one uninstantiated universal. Hence, if we accept Tooley's general line of argument, we must also accept that we could have good reasons for postulating uninstantiated universals. Uninstantiated universals are therefore logically possible.

One way which we could attempt to block this conclusion would be to deny that we can make sense of the notion of the absolutely or ontologically simple as applied to universals. But, with Tooley, I see no reason to deny the possibility of such simplicity. I do not know whether any simple universals actually exist. But I can see no reason to deny that they might exist.

Should we then simply accept the conclusion that it is logically possible that there are uninstantiated universals? This is the course which Tooley himself recommends. After all, mere logical possibilities are not very harmful. Nothing like Tooley's cases are to be found in current scientific approximations to the laws of nature. The Principle of Instantiation can be retained as a likely contingent truth.

However, I think that there is good reason to reject this approach. It will be a disaster for the theory of universals. Once the logical possibility of one universal existing uninstantiated is admitted, it seems difficult to deny the logical possibility of any universal existing uninstantiated. For is it to be supposed that universals will differ among themselves in this fundamental respect? Nor can the line be drawn at properties. For any relation also, it will have to be logically possible that it should exist without instantiation, that is, without terms. (It would not be difficult to construct Tooley cases involving relations rather than properties.) All universals will then become substances in Hume's sense, that is, things logically capable of independent existence.

120

But it seems mistaken to conceive of universals in this way. Without arguing the matter in detail here, I will say that there will be problems in connecting universals so conceived to their particulars. The problem is perhaps clearest in the case of relations. If a two-place relation holding between particulars *a* and *b* is something capable of independent existence apart from *a*, *b*, and other particulars, will it not require at least one further relation to link it to *a* and *b*? And if this relation can itself exist uninstantiated (as it would, for instance, in a universe of monads) it will be subject to the same infirmity, and so *ad infinitum*. This Bradleian regress can only be escaped if universals (and also the particularity of particulars) are mere abstract (but real) factors in states of affairs.

In any case, however, it seems that Tooley is forced to accept that there probably are *actual* uninstantiated universals. We have already seen that scientists do recognize the existence of various 'laws' which, although it is logically possible that they should be instantiated, are apparently uninstantiated. All such empirical cases seem to be cases of 'missing values' of more comprehensive functional laws. But they are uninstantiated laws nevertheless. Now what account is Tooley to give of the truth-makers for such laws? It will be extremely arbitrary for him to give a Realistic account of the 'laws' involved in his imaginary cases, yet give a non-Realistic account of those uninstantiated law-statements actually asserted by scientists. In consistency, he must postulate uninstantiated universals in the latter cases also. Then universals, however, will be actual, not merely possible.

So it seems that Tooley should include uninstantiated universals in his ontology. To those of us who wish to uphold the hypothesis that the only thing which in fact exists is the spatio-temporal manifold, this is an unwelcome conclusion. It gives us strong motive and reason for seeking an alternative account.

3 TOOLEY'S CASES SOLVED BY THE INTRODUCTION OF POWERS?

Tooley's cases, however, are an extremely rich source for metaphysical speculation. There is yet another way in which we can react when confronted by them. It would be possible to return to an old line of thought and to link universals with *powers*.

Suppose that it is a nomic truth that Fs which are *not* Gs cannot be Hs, and similarly that Gs which are *not* Fs cannot be Hs, but that it is a law that Fs which are also Gs are Hs. The universal, F, might then be thought to be linked to a *power*, possessed by all particulars which are F (G would have a similar power.) Whether the universal and the power are linked necessarily or contingently would be a further point for later discussion. But the things which were F would have a power, in virtue of being F, a power such that *if* they were also Gs, then they would further be Hs. *This* link between the power and its potential consequences would be necessary. (Things which were G would have a corresponding power.) In the simpler case where it was a law that Fs are Gs, Fs would presumably still have a power, but a full or plenary power which could not but be exercised.

How would this introduction of powers deal with Tooley's cases? Simply by saying that in Tooley-type cases what we would be dealing with would be *instantiated* universals which bestowed (non-plenary) powers upon the particulars which instantiated the universals. A B-type particle, for instance, might have the *power*, if it came to have R to a J-type particle, to produce some quite idiosyncratic upshot. A non-plenary power need not be exercised, and so it might be that this power never is exercised. There might also be other omnitemporally unexercised powers to produce something having a simple quality of a certain sort, a quality which no actual thing ever had or will have.

What the solution in terms of powers is doing is dealing with Tooley's uninstantiated laws by associating, as it were, a ghost of the consequent with the antecedent universals of the uninstantiated law. Having the power is very like having a mental state with an intentional object. Just as the intentional object may not be a real object, so the 'object' of the power may never be actualized. But the power still exists and points to its object. We have here a universalist equivalent of the objective propensities of particulars discussed in Chapter 3, Section 4. What was said there is relevant to the present discussion.

While granting that what we have here is a possible solution to the problem raised by Tooley's cases, I would wish to avoid, if at all possible, the cumbrous ontology of powers. We already have particulars and categorical universals, combined in states of affairs. To introduce powers is to introduce non-categorical universals alongside universals, and to introduce them in great profusion, wherever universals are linked by laws. Relations between universals will still be required. If an object instantiates a universal, then the universal bestows certain (universal) powers on the object. The relation between universal and powers may be necessary or it may be contingent. There is room for philosophical differences on this point. But there will be a *relation* between the two sorts of universal. Again there will apparently have to be some sort of relation between the power and its actualization, when the latter occurs. In such a case we have a plenary power, and the relation between power and actualization will be necessary.

Hence, since we will still require relations between universals, the ontology of powers is definitely uneconomical. This is a good reason for at least trying to see if we can proceed without powers.

A truly radical attempt to overcome the problem of linking categorical universals with powers would be to reduce all universals to powers. The properties of a thing would just be identified with the thing's capacities to act and be acted upon by other things.

I believe, however, that such an attempt is involved in vicious regress. The power is constituted the power it is by the *sort* of actualizations it gives rise to in suitable *sorts* of circumstance. But what are these sorts of actualization and sorts of circumstance? They themselves can be nothing but powers, and so again they can only be constituted by the sorts of actualization which they give rise to in suitable circumstances. The power to produce A is nothing but the power to produce the power to produce B . . . and so on. Nor will the situation be relieved by bringing the powers around in a circle.

4 A SCEPTICAL TREATMENT OF TOOLEY'S CASES

I therefore finally propose a sceptical account of Tooley's cases, a solution which does not accept one of Tooley's premisses. I begin from the already presented idea that statements of uninstantiated law are a certain sort of counterfactual. They are statements that *if* a certain universal was instantiated which in fact is not instantiated, then this universal would be related in a certain fashion to a certain other universal. The counterfactual is sustained by a statement of a higher-order law.

Let us identify these elements in Tooley's cases. In both of them we can point to, if not identify very precisely, the higher-order laws. In the Fundamental particle case we have the following. It is a law concerning the laws of 2-particle fundamental interactions that, given two different types of interaction (e.g. the A–A interaction and the B–D interaction) whatever (first-order) law governs the one interaction, then the first-order law governing the second type of interaction is quite different in form.

For the Emergent properties case we have the following sketch of a higher-order law. It is a law concerning a certain range of complex properties that, if objects have a certain sort of conjunction of properties in this range, then it is a law that they have certain emergent simple properties, a different simple property being associated with each different conjunction.

If there are no such higher-order laws, then, I maintain, there can be no uninstantiated laws. It is because the cases as sketched by Tooley suggest, as a best explanation of the given facts, that there are such higher-order laws, that he can go on to assert with plausibility the existence of his uninstantiated laws. If the latter are counterfactuals, as I am now suggesting, how else can they be sustained except by a higher-order law?

Suppose, now, that one has these higher-order laws as premisses, and that one conjoins them with the false premisses that B and J particles do sometimes meet (in the Fundamental particle case), or that the complex of properties S, T and U is somewhere co-instantiated (in the Emergent property case). One can then deduce that the B–J laws would be idiosyncratic. One can deduce that the conjunction of S, T and U would give rise to a new simple property. One can make statements of uninstantiated law, that is, assert a certain sort of counterfactual, to this effect.

Tooley's intuition, and it is a plausible one, is that, in such cases, there *is* a definite B–J interaction law, which we cannot know; and also that a certain definite simple property would emerge, although we cannot know what it would be. If this intuition is correct, then my resolution of his cases fails. But it is this intuition which I now wish to challenge.

My challenge is based upon certain reasonably widely appreciated features of counterfactual reasoning. Here is a more ordinary case of counterfactual reasoning (the details suggested by Gregory Currie). I think it weakens the grip of Tooley's cases.

Suppose that there is an irreducibly probabilistic law to the effect that, if P, then either Q or R will occur, but not both. Q and R are equiprobable. Suppose that a particular a, lacks property P at t, but suppose that it is nomically possible, although false, that it has P at t. It seems clear that, in this situation, we are entitled to assert the counterfactual: if *a* had been P at *t*, then either Q or R would have occurred. It is clear also that, since the law is *irreducibly* probabilistic, and the probabilities equal, that we have no reason to assert that the outcome would have been Q rather than R, or R rather than Q.

But suppose that a philosopher asserts: nevertheless, there is a truth of the matter. All that we are in a position to assert rationally is that the outcome would have been Q or R. Yet *in fact* the outcome would have been Q. Or it would have been R. Excluded middle holds. But our epistemological situation happens to be a little unfortunate.

For such a philosopher there are, besides actual states of affairs involving particulars, physically possible but non-actual states of affairs involving particulars. Since they are states of affairs, part of the ontological furniture, they are determinate. Excluded middle must hold. Against this, however, I suggest that, for the given case at least, this is an anti-Actualist stand which few of us would wish to take. The true position seems to be that there are no such states of affairs. There is no fact of the matter. Excluded middle fails.[1]

But now, in the light of this case, is it not quite plausible to treat Tooley's uninstantiated laws as the same sort of phenomenon, but one level higher up? We are certainly justified in asserting the counterfactual: if a B and a J were to interact, then the interaction would be governed by a quite idiosyncratic law. But this is simply a deduction from the higher-order laws governing laws of fundamental particle interaction in Tooley's universe, conjoined with a false premiss that B and J particles interact. There is no need to believe that there *is* a definite idiosyncratic law, but one, alas, forever unknown to us.

It must be admitted that there is some asymmetry of intuition here. In the first-order case, it is natural to think that excluded middle fails for the counterfactual involved. In Tooley's cases, it is quite natural, when presented with them, to think that the B–J combination of particles obey a definite but unknown law. Even considered in the light of the first-order case, Tooley's cases retain persuasive power.

I think that this asymmetry is linked to the tradition, as old as Plato, of treating particulars as contingent beings but universals as necessary ones. If a necessary being is possible, then it exists. If uni-

---

[1] In the now standard symbolism for counterfactuals, from $(P \square \rightarrow (Q \vee R))$ we cannot validly conclude that $((P \square \rightarrow Q) \vee (P \square \rightarrow R))$.

versals are necessary beings, therefore, every possible universal exists, though many may be uninstantiated. And if the universals exist, then they either have or do not have the relations attributed to them by Tooley.

I believe, however, that this is an incorrect philosophy of universals. Universals are as much contingent beings as particulars, and they do not exist uninstantiated. And so it becomes much less obvious that, if a universal that does not exist were to exist, that is, if a universal were instantiated, then it definitely would, or definitely would not, have certain relations to further universals.

I conclude, then, that Tooley's ingenious cases do not prevent us from treating statements of uninstantiated law as concealed counterfactuals, where truth or falsity depends wholly upon actual, that is, instantiated, laws. Statements of uninstantiated law assert only that if, contrary to fact, certain sorts of thing existed, then these things would obey a certain law. 'The law' may be specified indeterminately only, and have no being beyond this specification.

5 UNINSTANTIATED LAWS WITH NOMICALLY IMPOSSIBLE ANTECEDENTS

D. H. Mellor (1980, pp. 113–14) has pointed out that, in scientific practice, we sometimes assert the existence of 'laws' where the antecedent conditions are not merely uninstantiated, but are, and are understood by us to be, nomically impossible. His example is high temperature values of the vapour pressure law for water. The values are missing because it is a *law* that water decomposes before it reaches these temperatures.

As already pointed out in Chapter 2, Section 7, one can hardly admit as a genuine objective law one which has a nomically impossible antecedent. Here, then, is an uninstantiated law of which we certainly cannot give a Realistic account. We cannot possibly treat it as a law alongside other laws, but one happening to lack the characteristic of instantiation.

What account can we give of such laws? An account of the following sort seems more or less inevitable. The 'law' is deduced from a major and a minor premiss. The major premiss contains a certain law-statement presumed true, probably a functional law. But the major premiss also contains a contrary-to-fact assumption: that some further law of nature does not hold. The *holding* of this other law ensures that certain values of the variables in the original functional law are not instantiated. But with this other law 'thought away', these values become nomically possible. The minor premiss will then be the further false assumption that these forbidden values are actually instantiated. The conclusion of the argument will be that these values obey the formula of the first, functional, law. This conclusion, detached and asserted independently, constitutes the uninstantiated law.

Such statements of uninstantiated law are therefore counterfactuals about what law would hold if (a) a certain law did not hold; (b) a condition were instantiated which was made nomically possible by the fact that the law referred to in (a) did not hold. It is this condition which is governed by the uninstantiated 'law'.

There does not seem to be any particular difficulty here. But the result may be used as a further argument against any Realistic (e.g. Tooley-style) account of uninstantiated laws. As Mellor points out, scientific practice seems to make no very sharp distinction between uninstantiated laws which lack, and those which have, nomically possible antecedents. Now, since it seems that we have to give an anti-Realistic account of the former, this is some reason for giving an anti-Realistic account of *all* uninstantiated laws.

We will return to the subject of uninstantiated laws with nomically impossible antecedents when we discuss the view that laws of nature are logical necessities in nature (Ch. 11, Sec. 4).

9

Probabilistic laws

In the last two chapters we gave an account of functional laws as higher-order laws, that is, laws governing laws. We also proposed a (non-Realist) account of uninstantiated laws. Our next task is to try to bring irreducibly probabilistic laws within our scheme.

At first sight there appears to be some difficulty in this undertaking. Suppose it to be a law that Fs are Gs, and suppose that a is F. We then have:

(1) $(N(F,G))$ (a's being F, a's being G)

where $N(F,G)$ is a necessitation relation holding between the two states of affairs, a's being F and a's being G, a necessitation holding in virtue of the two universals involved in the two states of affairs.

Suppose, however, that the law which links F and G is irreducibly probabilistic. There is a probability $P(1 > P > O)$ that an F is a G. Suppose, again, that a is F. It would be simple and elegant to analyse the situation in just the same way as in the case of the deterministic law:

(2) $((Pr:P) (F,G))$ (a's being F, a's being G)

where $((Pr:P) (F,G))$ gives the objective probability of an F being a G, a probability holding in virtue of the universals F and G.

But, of course, there is an obvious difficulty. Because the law is only probabilistic, the state of affairs, a's being F, may not be accompanied by the state of affairs, a's being G. The 'relation' $((Pr:P) (F,G))$ will then lack its second term.

How might we try to get round this failure of symmetry?

First, it might be suggested that the probabilistic law can be instantiated by two different sorts of situation:

(3) $((Pr:P) (F,G))$ (a's being F, a's being G)
(4) $((Pr:1-P) (F,G))$ (a's being F, a's not being G).

The difficulty with this view is that it involves postulating negative states of affairs, in order to provide a second term for the relation in (4). It may be that a satisfactory metaphysics is forced to postulate such states of affairs, but we should certainly try to avoid doing so if at all possible. Absences and lacks are ontologically suspect. (If absences and lacks are real, why, if there is a choice between the presence of A and the absence of A, should Occam's Razor disfavour the former?)

Second, we might re-introduce chances or propensities within the states of affairs:

(5) $(N(F,H))$ (a's being F, a's being H)

with H a P-strength propensity to be G. This has the advantage that we do not need the new universals of the form $(Pr:P)$ (F,G), but can instead appeal to universals of the form of our old friend $(N(F,G))$. Its disadvantage is equally obvious: we are back with propensities or powers as extra, irreducible, properties of individuals, over and above the categorical properties.

I think that we have a better way out than either of the two suggestions just noted. I suggest that we can after all stick with the original suggestion:

(2) $((Pr:P)$ $(F,G))$ (a's being F, a's being G).

What we must do, though, is limit the instantiation of the universal $((Pr:P)$ $(F,G))$ to those cases where the particular which is F is also G. *Probabilistic laws are universals which are instantiated only in the cases where the probability is realized.*

One objection to the suggestion is obvious. What if, omnitemporally, the probability is never realized? Given the rejection of uninstantiated universals, this would mean that there was no law. Yet does not the probabilistic law itself provide for the *physical* possibility that every instance falling under the law is a negative instance?

I wish to deny this possibility. If there is to be a law giving a probability that Fs are Gs, then, I assert, it is logically necessary that, at some time, there exists an F which is a G instantiating the law. The situation is the same as that with ordinary universals. If the monadic universal, U, is to exist, then it is not necessary that any specific particular have property U. But it is necessary that, at some time, there be a particular which has U. Otherwise U can be no more than a merely logically possible universal, or, at best, a merely physically possible universal.

Suppose that Fs are never Gs. If we say that nevertheless there could be a probabilistic law giving a chance of Fs being G, then, given that laws of nature are relations between universals, we shall have to allow that the universal G exists. But G may not be instantiated. For it seems absurd that the existence of the F→G law depends upon the existence of Gs *elsewhere*, Gs which have nothing to do with Fs. So we are back with the logical possibility of uninstantiated universals, a possibility rejected in the previous chapter.

But having said these things, we are now in a position to qualify them. Although we have rejected uninstantiated universals and uninstantiated laws (a particular case of uninstantiated universals) as items in the universe alongside instantiated universals and laws, we have allowed that *statements* of uninstantiated law may have more or less objective truth-conditions. As a result, it can be allowed in the case under discussion that no Fs might be Gs, and yet that a 'law' might still be truly assertable giving a certain probability of an F being a G.

Uninstantiated law-statements, I have argued, are, if properly understood, a species of counterfactual. They tell us only what laws would hold if, contrary to fact, certain universals were instantiated. They are counterfactuals which require to be backed by further laws: higher-order laws. Suppose, then, that the property F has the property P. And suppose that all other properties besides F which have the property P bestow upon their particulars a certain identical probability of being a G, a probability which is actually realized in some cases associated with each property. We have a series of (instantiated) probabilistic laws, all having the same form.

Under these circumstances, it would be reasonable to explain (unify) this series of laws by postulating a higher-order law to the effect that *any* P-type property involved a first-order law to the effect that such a property bestowed on its particulars a certain fixed probability of being a G. Given the law, it could then be deduced for the case of Fs that, despite the fact that none of them were Gs, they too had that probability of being a G. (Perhaps the probability was rather low, and the omnitemporal number of Fs rather small.) The probabilistic F-law could then be thought of as a universal which was omnitemporally never instantiated (and which therefore did not exist), but which had a *physical* possibility (indeed, a certain probability) of existing.

By contrast, suppose that no Fs are Gs, and that no higher-order law exists from which it could be deduced that Fs have some probability of being a G. Then, I maintain, it cannot be the case that there is in any sense a law that Fs have a certain probability of being a G.

Is this conclusion counterintuitive? I do not think it is seriously so. It is clear that in such circumstances we would have no *reason* to assert a law giving Fs a probability of being a G. (The situation would not be like the Tooley cases, where an elaborate scenario was outlined which did give an apparent reason to assert an uninstantiated law. Such a scenario gives just the sort of evidence which would make us suspect the presence of a higher-order law, and the higher-order law can in turn be used to justify 'uninstantiated laws'.) In the interest of getting rid of those strange entities: uninstantiated laws and uninstantiated universals: I suggest that we take this lack of reason to have not merely an epistemological but also an ontological moral. Real laws, like all real universals, are instantiated in space-time.

It may be noted, incidentally, that there is no parallel difficulty where a merely probabilistic law linking Fs and Gs is instantiated in *each* case. This might even be a likely happening where the probability was high and the omnitemporal number of Fs low. Yet the law could still be genuinely probabilistic, not deterministic. There would be a problem how we could *tell* that it was only a probabilistic law. But even here we might have rather good evidence to show that it was not deterministic. For instance, it might be that we were *forced* to postulate merely probabilistic laws in other cases because they all involved actual cases where probabilities failed to be realized. This would be evidence for a higher-order law that *all* the relevant laws were probabilistic, even those whose manifestations were compatible with their being deterministic.

2 PROBABILISTIC LAWS AS PROBABILITIES OF NECESSITATION

If probabilistic laws are only instantiated in those cases where the probability is realized, then the way is open, at least, to think of such laws as involving necessitation. Let it be a law that Fs have a certain probability of being a G. Let *a* be F and be G, and let this state of affairs be an instantiation of the law. We have:

(1) $((Pr:P) (F,G))$ (a's being F, a's being G).

I should like to read this as saying that a's being F *necessitates* a's being G, a necessitation holding in virtue of the fact that universals F and G give a certain probability, P, of such a necessitation. Instead of formula (1) we might restore our relation N and write:

(2) $((N:P) (F, G))$ (a's being F, a's being G)

where P is a number between 1 and 0, including infinitesimals. If the law had been deterministic, where we previously wrote:

(3) $(N(F,G))$ (a's being F, a's being G)

we could now rewrite (3) as a limiting case of (2):

(4) $((N:1) (F,G))$ (a's being F, a's being G).

It is to be noted that the necessitation involved here is necessitation in the singular case: a's being F necessitating a's being G. As we have already seen in Chapter 6, Section 5, in discussing Miss Anscombe's view, it is intelligible that the necessitation should be *purely* singular: without benefit of law. But necessitation in the singular case can also hold in virtue of a relation of universals. If the relation between F and G is (N:1) then there logically must be necessitation in each singular case. If the relation is (N:P) where P is less than 1, then we have a certain objective probability of necessitation in each singular case.

I now offer four arguments, none of them conclusive but all I think suggestive, in favour of an interpretation of probabilistic laws as giving a probability of a necessitation.

The first consideration arises from thinking about *causal* laws. We generally conceive of these as deterministic, but this seems just a habit of thought. The laws could be irreducibly probabilistic. Suppose physicalism is true, and that the laws of physics are irreducibly indeterministic, as the quantum laws appear to be. Belief in such premisses would surely not lead us to deny that there were causes of the French Revolution. Rather we should say that it did have causes, but causes governed by irreducibly probabilistic laws.

Now consider a case where a cause, a singular event, brings about its effect, a further singular event, but the sequence is governed by an irreducibly probabilistic law. The first event *caused*, brought

132

about, the second event. If so, did it not necessitate the second event? Is not causing a species of necessitation? Yet the law governing the sequence was probabilistic. So the probabilistic law gives a probability of a necessitation, a probability which was realized in this case.

A second line of thought which inclines me in the same direction is due to Michael Tooley (unpublished to date). Suppose that it is an irreducibly probabilistic law that if a G has property E, then there is a 50/50 chance that, as a result, the G will have property H. It is also an irreducibly probabilistic law that if a G has the property F, then there is a 50/50 chance that, as a result, the G will have the property H. It is physically possible for a G to be *both* an E and an F at the same time. Finally, it is only by being an E or an F that a G can be an H.

Now suppose that, on a certain occasion, *a*, which is a G, has the properties E *and* F. It is also an H.

What should we say about this case? Should we simply say that, because *a* was E and F, it had an increased chance of being H, a chance which was realized? It seems to me, as it seems to Tooley, that it is natural to want to say *more* than this. It is natural to ask whether it is *a*'s being E, or *a*'s being F, or perhaps both (a case of overdetermination), which is *responsible* for *a*'s being H. But to talk this way is to suggest that it was (1) *a*'s being E; *or* (2) *a*'s being F; *or* (3) both; which *necessitated a*'s being H.[1]

There appear to be three sets of counterfactuals associated with the three possibilities. (1′) If *a* had still been E, but had not been F, it would still have been H. If *a* had been F, but not E, it would not have been H. (2′) If *a* had been F, but had not been E, it would still have been H. If *a* had been E, but not F, it would not have been H. (3′) Only if *a* had not been E and not been F would it not have been H.

These three sets of counterfactuals, (1′) (2′) and (3′), are incompatible. If one accepts that one of them is true (although it is by bad chance impossible to tell which), and further accepts the plausible principle that the truth-maker for the true set is some categorical feature of the world, then this truth-maker is naturally identified as a pattern of necessitation.[2]

---

[1] A similar case, from which a similar moral is drawn, is proposed by John Foster (1979, pp. 169–70).

[2] In Ch. 8, Sec. 4, it was argued that if it is a law that where P, then either Q or R, but

A third consideration is this. We reach the same result, *viz.* that probabilistic laws give a probability of a necessitation, if we think of the probabilistic laws involved as universals, universals instantiated only in the cases where the probabilities are somewhere realized. If, in the cases just discussed, the GE→H law applies to the case of *a*, we have:

(1) $((N:.5) ((E\&G),H))$ (*a*'s being E&G, *a*'s being H).

In words, this may be rendered: the state of affairs of *a*'s being both E and G necessitates *a*'s being H, a necessitation holding in virtue of the fact that the universals involved $((E\&G),H)$ give a probability of such a necessitation of .5. If the GF→H law applies to the case of *a* we have:

(2) $((N:.5) ((F\&G),H))$ (*a*'s being F&G, *a*'s being H)

with a parallel translation. At least one of these law-universals must apply to the case, linking the states of affairs named inside the right-hand parenthesis of each formula. As already anticipated in my translation of (1), what can these links be but necessitations?

Fourthly, and finally, another idea of Tooley's pushes us in the same direction. Suppose that it is an irreducibly probabilistic law that Fs have a certain probability of being Gs. But suppose that there is indeterminism in the universe, and some Fs are Gs not because they instantiate a law, but for no reason at all. The joint satisfaction of these two conditions seems to be a meaningful supposition. Suppose now that *a* is F and is G. Is this case a manifestation of the

without any factor to determine whether it is Q or R which obtains, then the counterfactual 'if *a* were P, then *a* would be Q or R' is sustained, but it cannot be concluded that if *a* were P, then *a* would be Q or *a* would be R. There is no inconsistency between this stand and our present contention that, since we are able to assert different and incompatible counterfactuals about the conditions under which the G would not have been H, different patterns of necessitation correspond to the different counterfactuals. In the former case, it is natural to assert that *a* would be Q or R, but not at all natural to assert that either *a* would be Q, or, *a* would be R, although we cannot know which. We simply do not think that there are such counterfactual facts. But in our present case it seems *natural* to assert that one of three incompatible sets of counterfactuals is true, although we cannot tell which. It is therefore reasonable to look for incompatible categorical truth-makers to correspond to these incompatible counterfactuals. I suggest that we find these truth-makers in different patterns of necessitation. In the former case we would be arguing to counterfactuals – on the basis of excluded middle – counterfactuals whose truth-maker does not easily appear. In the latter case we are arguing from counterfactuals which it is natural to assert to a categorical truth-maker.

probabilistic law, or is it simply an indeterministic phenomenon? If this question can be meaningfully asked, as it seems that it can, then we give an account of the distinction by saying that in the first case *a*'s being F *necessitates* *a*'s being G, a necessity absent in the second case. The necessitation, in turn, is an instantiation of the probabilistic law.

One thing which might worry one in this account of probabilistic laws is whether Actualism has been deserted. Are we not involved in irreducible potentialities, which are rejected in other places in this book? Take the case where it is a probabilistic law that Fs are G, this law is instantiated in a number of cases, and then consider *a*, an F which is not G. Object *a* has a certain probability, P, of being G, but the probability is not realized. Is not this probability a pure unrealized potentiality of *a* to be G?

I trust that this is not so. I want to say that *a* is F, that it has various other categorical properties, and that that is the end of the matter as far as *a* is concerned. It is certainly true that *a* had a certain probability of being G. But the truth-maker for this truth is to be found in the positive instantiations of the probabilistic law. And what is to be found in the positive instantiations is the instantiation of a certain objective relation between the universals F and G: the relation (N:P) (F,G).

3 OTHER TYPES OF PROBABILISTIC LAWS

In the probabilistic law which we have been considering, each F is quite independent of every other F in respect of its having the property G. But we can conceive of laws having a probabilistic element where this is not so. For instance, it could be a law that a certain proportion of the Fs all existing at one time are Gs. This condition is not probabilistic. But it might be added that the Fs which are Gs do not differ in any nomically relevant way from the Fs which are not G. Yet a certain proportion nomically must be Gs.

Such a law would not be a law governing individual Fs but governing more sophisticated individuals: for instance, the class of Fs at a time. It would be necessitated that a certain proportion of the members of all such classes were Gs. The law-statement would sustain counterfactuals of a sort which a straightforward probabilistic law-statement would not sustain. We could say, for instance, 'This F, which is G, might not have been G (nomically might not), but if it had not been G, then some other (unspecified) F among the F non-Gs would have been a G.'

If there are metaphysical qualms about classes (as I believe that there should be) then it may be possible to substitute for talk about the class of Fs at a time the aggregate of the Fs at that time. Consider the aggregate of the Fs at a time. There will always be one and only one way of dividing that aggregate into two parts, so that the two parts have the following nature. The first part can be exhaustively and exclusively divided into parts each of which is an F which is a G. The second part can be similarly divided into parts each of which is an F which is not a G. The first part will be a structure of, say M F-parts. The second part will be a structure of, say N F-parts. The numerical relationship M/N reflects the proportion of Fs which are Gs in the whole class of Fs at a given time. To say that a certain proportion of the Fs at any time nomically must be Gs is to say that the M/N ratio cannot fall below a certain value V. In this way, perhaps, the law can be represented as a law about the aggregate of the Fs at a time. A proportion, V, of the F-parts of the aggregate of the Fs must be Gs.

10

Further considerations concerning the form of laws

After introducing the conception of laws of nature both as relations holding between universals, and as universals, in Chapter 6, we tried in the next three chapters to extend the account to functional laws, to uninstantiated laws and to probabilistic laws. It was argued that functional laws are higher-order laws: laws which dictate, or in some possible cases merely govern, lower-order laws. It was argued that uninstantiated laws are not really laws at all, but are rather counterfactuals about what laws would hold if certain conditions were realized. In the case of probabilistic laws it was argued that our original schema can be applied fairly straightforwardly. Such laws give probabilities of necessitation, probabilities less than probability 1. Deterministic laws are laws where the probability of necessitation is 1.

There are a great many other questions to be considered concerning the possible forms which a law of nature can take. In this chapter various of these issues will be taken up.

1 SCIENTIFIC IDENTIFICATION

We may begin from the point that, if our general account of laws of nature is to be sustained, they must contain at least two universals. What then of theoretical identifications, such as the identification of temperature with mean kinetic energy, or laws of universal scope, that is, laws having the form: it is a law that everything is F? The present section will be devoted to theoretical identification.

Consider the identification of water with H_2O, temperature with mean kinetic energy, inertial mass with gravitational mass. Are they laws of nature? They are certainly purely general scientific truths, discovered *a posteriori*. (It is a matter of current dispute whether they are necessary or contingent truths. I favour the latter view, but the matter need not be argued here.) If water is H_2O, to

137

take this as our example, then we have two universally quantified generalizations: all samples of water are made up of H_2O molecules, all collections of H_2O molecules are samples of water. Is it *laws* which are instantiated in each instance falling under the generalizations? It is interesting to notice that, given the Molnar definition of the Regularity theory of laws of nature (Ch. 2, Sec. 1), and given further that the generalizations are contingent, the generalizations qualify as laws of nature. For they are universally quantified, omnitemporally and omnispatially true, and, besides logical terms, contain nothing but non-logical predicates.[1]

Some think of these identifications as laws, for instance, Mellor, 1978, pp. 119–20. Pap spoke of 'composition laws' (1962, p. 363), Fodor speaks of 'bridge laws' (1974).[2]

But if we accept a Realistic theory of properties (universals), and hold that laws are relationships between these properties, then for these 'identifications' to be laws they would have to link distinct properties. The distinct predicates would have to apply in virtue of distinct properties. And, indeed, it is conceivable that, for instance, temperature and mean kinetic energy of molecules are distinct co-extensive properties. But every principle of method speaks for their being the same property. However, if the identifications are genuine identifications, then, given our view of laws, they cannot be laws.

Is this embarrassing? I do not think so. They are not very plausible cases of laws. There is, however, a rather shallow dialectic which can drive us to thinking that they must be laws. It is rather easy to endorse unthinkingly the reflection that the discoveries of natural science are *confined* to: (1) the laws of nature; (2) matters of historical and geographical fact (in the widest sense of 'history' and 'geography'). It is a reflection which I myself have endorsed in the past. If this is in the back of one's mind, then one will find general scientific identifications puzzling. They are certainly not mere his-

---

[1] David Lewis has suggested to me that here is another difficulty for the Naive Regularity theory. It is certainly clear that it is a difficulty for the Molnar definition. But a Naive Regularity theory could meet the objection in at least one way: by accepting universals, and then stipulating that in a formula such as '$(x) (Fx \supset Gx)$', 'F' and 'G' should name *distinct* universals. As has several times been pointed out, this stipulation would also serve to dissolve the grue problem.

[2] Fodor, in his article, is critical of the idea that certain bridge-laws exist, in particular that there are bridge-laws between psychology and physics. But he does not challenge the *conception* of bridge-laws.

torical or geographical facts. The temptation is then to try to see them as laws of nature.

But if the position taken up in this essay is anywhere near correct, then we can already see that this dichotomy is too simple. For there is at least one other task which science has: the identification of genuine universals (genuine properties and relations). It is true that establishing what universals there are is inextricably bound up with establishing what the laws of nature are. But the enterprises are still distinguishable. After all, establishing the laws, on the one hand, and the historical and geographical facts, on the other, are enterprises which are also inextricably bound up with each other. Yet they are clearly distinguishable enterprises.

What, then, are scientific identifications? I think that they are a matter of discovering truths about universals, but not those truths which constitute the laws of nature. It is a discovery about temperature that it is mean kinetic energy, but it is not a *law* about temperature. Rather, we have made a discovery about the internal structure of the universal, or class of universals, *temperature*. It may be compared to the discovery of the internal structure of a certain particular object, for instance, the internal structure of the Earth. But instead of exploring the geography of a first-order particular, the Earth, we are instead exploring the geography of a second-order particular: the universal of temperature. Most universals are complex, conceivably all are ('structures all the way down'). Science is concerned, among other things, to lay out the internal structure of universals.

The above account seems to fit the case of water and of temperature. The identification of inertial and gravitational mass is not quite the same. It is instead the second-order equivalent of identifying a certain mountain seen from one perspective, with a certain mountain seen from another, or, indeed, with identifying Hesperus with Phosphorus. Property A, inertial mass, is known in one way, as a universal figuring in a certain set of laws or putative laws. Property B, gravitational mass, is known in another way, as a universal figuring in a different set of laws or putative laws. They turn out to be (are hypothesized to be) the very same universal.

A less sophisticated but similar case is that where visually apprehended roundness (the seen shape of coins, saucers, etc.) is identified with tactually apprehended roundness (the felt shape of coins, saucers, etc.). One philosopher who resists this identification is Berkeley. He maintains in the *New Theory of Vision* that the objects of sight and touch are not merely *numerically* different (although he thinks they are) but *specifically* different also (Sec. 121–48). Most of us, however, take the 'two' roundnesses to be one and the same property.

2 LAWS WITH UNIVERSAL SCOPE

Scientific identifications do not really seem to raise any problem for our account of laws. But, as Tooley has pointed out (1977, pp. 676–7), a real problem is set by laws with universal scope: laws of the form, everything is F. It is not clear that any such laws actually obtain. But it is clearly possible that there should be such laws. How could they be relations between universals? They can hardly involve a universal necessitating itself!

It may be noted, incidentally, that here is one of the few places where the Regularity theory, and equally any theory which simply places some necessity operator in front of the Regularity formulae but makes no attempt to explicate that operator in terms of relations between universals, has a clear advantage over our theory. There is no *special* problem about a regularity with universal scope. Those of us who reject the Regularity theory would point out that that theory cannot draw the apparently intelligible distinction between accidental and law-like regularities with universal scope. But this is simply a particular case of the general difficulty that the Regularity theory has in drawing the accidental/law-like distinction among regularities.

We have admitted, as a primitive, the notion of necessitation: one state of affairs necessitating another. Kicked upstairs to universals this becomes the notion of a certain sort of state of affairs necessitating another: one universal necessitating another. In both these cases we have a dyadic notion of necessitation. Could there be a primitive *monadic* notion of necessitation also, and could this be appealed to explain laws of universal scope?

As Peter Forrest has pointed out, such a solution would gain plausibility if we could give sense to notions of triadic, tetradic . . . *n*-adic necessitation also.

However, I do not believe that this solution is a possible one. Consider the anti-Realist view of laws that they are mere inference-licences. The Realist will reject this. But the Realist will surely not reject the view that laws supply an ontological ground which, being known or hypothesized, licenses an inference. It seems, furthermore, that in *every* case a law licenses an inference. Given a law, we can always use it to specify a certain sort of state of affairs which, if given together with the law, allows us to infer to a further state of affairs. (We may, of course, only be able to infer a certain probability that the further state of affairs obtains or will obtain.) However complex the first state of affairs may be, the law must respect the dyadic structure of that inference. In such an inference we go from what can always be represented as *a* premiss to a conclusion. It seems that the law should have a corresponding dyadic structure because, if it did not, it could not be used to make these inferences. (This is the justification for talking of the universals involved in a law as 'antecedent' and 'consequent' universals.) The point holds even for the case of laws of universal scope. Given that something exists, it can be inferred that it is F. So nomic necessitation must always be dyadic.

One rather disreputable way to solve our problem would be to treat a law of universal scope as a cosmological version of Smith's garden. All the fruit in Smith's garden must be apples. All the things in the world must be Fs. In the first case, it was suggested (Ch. 6, Sec. 7), we have a relation between what we called a quasi-universal: *being a fruit grown in Smith's garden* and a universal *being an apple*. In the second case we have a relation between *being anything in the universe* and *being F*. The universe is here taken as a particular – as a very big garden indeed.

However, Tooley has suggested another, considerably more elegant, way out (1977, p. 676). We could take the law with universal scope to be a higher-order law. The higher-order law would read thus. It is a law concerning properties that, if something has any property, P, then it is a (first-order) law that Ps are Fs. *Being a property* nomically necessitates that something's having that property nomically necessitates that something being F.

To carry through this solution involves maintaining that *being a property* is itself a property: a second-order property possessed by properties. For, after all, we do not just want the second-order Humean uniformity that, for every property, it is a law that if something has that property, it further has F. That is no more than the *manifestation* of the second-order law. Instead, we want property-hood to be nomically active in the situation. Fortunately, it seems plausible to argue that propertyhood is a genuine property of properties. (As already argued, independently of the current issue, in Armstrong, 1978, Ch. 23, Sec. III.) It is not simply the case that the predicate 'property' applies to all properties.

Given the rather simple nature of the manifestation of a law of universal scope – everything is F – this solution seems a trifle cumbrous and elaborate. It also involves overdetermination. If a thing has more than one property, then it will have F in virtue of *each* of these properties.

A third solution has been suggested to me by Peter Forrest. We need first to notice that talk about laws of universal scope can hardly be taken literally. If the scope is to be truly universal, then every existent, be it particular or universal of any order, law, state of affairs or whatever, will have to have the property F. But there can hardly be laws of this sort. A 'law of universal scope' will have to be more restricted than this. Its form might be:

Every first–order particular is an F,

although, in view of the different sorts of particular which we recognize (thing, event, process, etc.), even this might be too wide. Let us, however, remain with this form.

Now consider that each first-order particular may be said to have something in common which marks it off from all other existents: the property of *first-order particularity*. How seriously we should take this property is not at all clear. If there were no question of laws of universal scope, then one might argue that here we have a mere predicate to which no genuine property, no genuine universal, corresponds. But universals are to be postulated *a posteriori*. If there appears to be a law that every first-order particular has property F, then might we not attribute nomic power to first-order particulars *in their character as first-order particulars*? Being a first-order particular necessitates being F. But to construe the law in this way is to introduce a genuine monadic universal of *being a first-order particular*.

I will not attempt to adjudicate between Tooley's and Forrest's solutions of the problem about laws of universal scope. Both of them seem to be reasonably promising ways of solving the problem.

But before leaving this section I will say something about Determinism. We may perhaps formulate the hypothesis of Determinism in the following way. For every (first-order) universal, there exists a deterministic (strictly universal) law, such that the universal is the consequent universal in that law. Such a formulation fits in with our general approach. Now, as Tooley has pointed out, we have to distinguish between it being a fact, that for every universal that universal is the consequent universal in a law, and it being a *law* that this is so. The fact could obtain although the law did not obtain. The fact could be a 'cosmic coincidence' concerning universals, a mere universal quantification.

If Determinism is a law, then, it will have to be a second-order law, a law that certain laws exist, and, linking up with the concerns of this section, it will be a law of universal scope, that is, a law about *all* first-order universals. What will the form of the law be? I think it will be something like this:

N (*being a first-order universal, being N-ed by a (first-order) universal*).

Once again, although we should not assume *a priori* that *being a first-order universal* is a universal, if we think that there are good scientific reasons to believe that Determinism is a law, then we would have *a posteriori* reasons to postulate the existence of this second-order universal. *Being N-ed by a (first-order) universal*, that is, *having the converse of N to some (first-order) universal*, has the form of a relational property which might attach to universals. There is no reason to deny that relational properties are real, nor to deny that they could be terms of a N relation (for this, see Sec. 6 of the present chapter).

A weaker hypothesis than Determinism is that, for each first-order universal, there exists some law, deterministic *or* probabilistic, such that the universal is the consequent universal in some law. Everything is governed, but not necessarily governed by deterministic laws. We might call this Weak Determinism. Whether Strong Determinism is true, or even whether Weak Determinism is true is, I take it, not a matter to be decided *a priori* by philosophers.

3 ARE THERE ANY EXCLUSION LAWS?

If we reject negative properties, as I am inclined to think that we should, then exclusion laws involve some difficulty. Consider the putative law that Fs cannot be Gs. If *not being G* is not a property, then it cannot be the case that F-ness necessitates the presence of this property in F-particulars. An exclusion law, then, will have to be a matter of a relation between F and the universal G. If we accept the Principle of Instantiation, the latter will have to be instantiated elsewhere.

In my 1978 (Ch. 24, Sec. II) I simply accepted exclusion laws under these conditions. But subsequent reflection shows how unsatisfactory the account is. What have instances of G at other times and places got to do with the exclusion law? In any case, if there are exclusion laws, there seems no call for the excluded property to be instantiated. Suppose, for instance, that, given certain conditions, a law forbids a certain arrangement of fundamental particles. Why should that arrangement be somewhere else instantiated?

Furthermore, if the view outlined in Chapter 6 is accepted, that laws of nature are not simply relations between universals but are at the same time universals themselves, instantiated in their instances, then the exclusion law certainly cannot be a relation between F and G. Consider a particular instantiation: a is F, and a's being F excludes a's being G. There is here no *being* G to be related to. We must either accept *not being* G as a universal, attaching to a, or else reject the possibility of exclusion laws.

One way to deal with this problem would be to accept the existence of negative universals on a selective basis only. It is the reverse of scientific to postulate negative universals in automatic fashion wherever the positive universal is absent. For, in general, such absences do no work in the world, and their postulation does no work in our theories. But if negative universals are postulated selectively, for instance, where they are required for exclusion laws, then it may be possible to live with them in good Empiricist conscience. So we can consider the *selective* relaxation of the ban on negative universals.

However, let us also explore more bold policies. Do we really need exclusion laws? Let us begin by considering the general problem of negative facts or states of affairs. It seems that if we know every positive fact about the world, then given that these are the totality of positive facts, we are deductively given every negative fact. Negative facts appear to be supervenient upon the positive facts, which suggests that they are nothing more than the positive facts. Given a true negative statement, the truth-makers for this statement are positive states of affairs.

Suppose, then, that we are given the totality of positive laws,

144

deterministic and probabilistic. If we then take the totality of possible worlds in which these and only these laws obtain, we are given all the positive physical possibilities among particular states of affairs. Now, it may be suggested, do not these positive physical possibilities give us all the physical possibilities? What need of further exclusion laws? The latter are supervenient upon the positive possibilities. It might be useful in practice to have exclusion formulae. But these will do no more than tell us where the positive possibilities have their limits.

But might it not be that among the physical possibilities allowed by the *positive* laws alone, there would be certain arrangements which nomically could not arise? To take account of these, it may be argued, it would be necessary to include exclusion laws in addition. However, it seems that it should be possible to accommodate the exclusions indirectly, by putting some *positive* modification or qualification into the positive laws. One could try to take advantage of an old line of thought about negations. Suppose Fs to be Hs, where H is a positive property (say, having a certain velocity). What is H is of necessity not-G (having another velocity). In attributing positive H to an F, one is automatically attributing the negative not-G. So one could try to represent the nomic exclusion of a certain arrangement as the nomic permitting of a certain positive arrangement, or range of positive arrangements, where the positive arrangements *logically* exclude the excluded arrangements.

At this point, it will be useful to introduce a distinction among types of law which is of considerable importance for our argument as a whole, but which will also cast light on the particular topic of exclusion laws. This is the distinction between *underived* laws and *derived* laws. Underived laws are what we have hitherto spoken of as laws. They are relations between universals. Derived laws are mere logical consequences of the holding of underived laws. Suppose that all the underived laws are given, together with the premiss that these are all the underived laws. Whatever further nomic truths can be deduced from this body of truths constitute the derived laws. The vital point is that they involve no new relations between universals.

We can now say that, in the situation envisaged in the penultimate paragraph, given it is an (underived) deterministic law that Fs are H (which is positive), and that H logically excludes G, then it is a *derived* exclusion law that no Fs are Gs. But we need

145

not object to derived, but only to *underived*, exclusion laws.

It would be possible for this device to lead to a certain artificiality. Suppose, for example, that the world was apparently governed by just one functional law, but that a certain few values of the function appeared not to be permitted. It would be necessary to recast the function so that its positive range of permitted values did not include the forbidden values. This might be conspicuously more artificial than combining the original function with a few underived exclusion principles.

A further case where it may seem even more difficult to resist underived exclusion principles is this. Suppose that the world is lawless and that properties are found attaching to particulars in almost every possible collocation. One combination, however, never occurs: no Fs are Gs. This could just be cosmic accident. But could it not also be the manifestation of an underived exclusion law?

The putative situation is an extreme and peculiar one. But giving an account of it in terms of positive laws would be rather uneconomical. It would be necessary to postulate laws for every property, giving some probability that a particular having that property had any other property. Only one such law would be lacking: a law which gave an F a probability of being a G. In such a situation we might prefer to postulate a single underived exclusion law.

In any case, David Lewis has objected, is there any reason to assume, as is here assumed, that indeterminism must involve a distribution of definite probabilities? Might it not be that there are no laws at all, except that exclusion law?

Suppose this apparent exclusion law to be that no Fs are Gs. One might still explain the facts without involving an underived exclusion law by postulating a positive property, H, such that H logically excludes the property G, and such that it is a law that Fs are Hs. But can we say that in such a case such a positive H *must* exist?

The upshot of this discussion is that there are *perhaps* situations where one would wish to introduce underived exclusion principles as genuine connections between universals. But, if this has to be done, it seems important to do this by introducing negative properties, and make the law a matter of some positive state of affairs necessitating a negative property. We introduce a new type of property rather than a new type of law. For only thus can the law be treated as instantiated in its instances.

If we do have selectively to introduce negative properties we can distinguish between negative states of affairs (a particular's having a negative property) necessita*ting* and negative states of affairs being necessita*ted*. It seems that while we ought to be reluctant to introduce necessitated negative states of affairs, we should be extremely reluctant to countenance necessitating negative states of affairs. Lacks and absences could perhaps be thought of as effects, but we ought to be deeply reluctant to think of them as causes.

In this section, at any rate, it will be assumed that there are no negative necessitating conditions. Given this premiss, it will be argued that we can then draw an interesting and important distinction between types of law. Our argument looks back to the discussion of infinitely qualified laws in Chapter 3, Section 3.

Suppose it to be a nomic truth that, with an exception, Fs are Gs. Let the exception be that Fs which are Hs are not Gs. Consider now *a* which is an F, but not an H. *a*'s being F necessitates that *a* is G, and necessitates it in virtue of the universals involved. By hypothesis, these universals do not include *not being H*. Notice, however, that although *a*'s being F necessitates *a*'s being G, it is not the case that each F is a G. We have:

(1) $((N:1) (F,G))$ (*a*'s being F, *a*'s being G)

but we do *not* have:

(2) $(x) (Fx \supset Gx)$.

Contrast this with the case where *a*'s being F necessitates *a*'s being G, and F and G are such that *a*'s being F necessitates *a*'s being G *whatever other properties a has*. In this second case (2) is true – *each* F is a G.

Following a suggestion by J. W. N. Watkins (in correspondence) I shall call laws of the second sort 'iron' laws. They tell us that, given certain conditions, some further state of affairs is necessitated (or has a certain probability of being necessitated – note that an iron law can be irreducibly probabilistic) no matter what further conditions are added. If it is a case of necessitation (N:1), then the law issues in an exceptionless uniformity.

It will now be seen that the analysis of laws given in Chapter 6 is an analysis of iron laws. But we also need to recognize that there can be laws which are less than iron laws, and which therefore need not issue in exceptionless uniformities. Following a suggestion by Ann Dix, I shall call them 'oaken' laws. David Lewis suggested 'rubber' laws to me, but this is potentially misleading because too soft. Oaken laws can be deterministic laws. Given *a* is F, and given that H is absent, *a* nomically must be G. Indeed, it seems that every law could be an oaken law, and yet Determinism be true of the universe, although there would have to be an infinite number of laws, since every law would have to be qualified.

The oaken law which we have considered has associated with it a single factor which, if present, will prevent an F being a G. But it is not contrary to reason that there should be an infinite number of factors such as H, factors lacking any common factor but each preventing an F from being what it naturally tends to be in the absence of interfering factors: a G.

It seems to be a contingent matter whether the laws of our universe are all iron, all oaken or are a mixture of the two. It has been suggested, for instance, that the law of the disintegration of the radium atom, like other quantum laws, is a probabilistic *but iron* law. Under all physically possible circumstances, there is the same objective probability that, over a certain time-interval, the atom will disintegrate.

Consider by way of contrast Newton's First Law. A body continues in its present state of motion or rest unless acted upon by a force. (Let us assume, for the sake of the case, that the law is an *instantiated* law. Perhaps the forces upon a particular particle exactly balance for a period of time, producing at least a simulacrum of the antecedent of the law.) Here the present state of the body is *determined* by its previous state to continue in that previous state: we might think of it as a case of immanent causation. But the law is oaken. As explicitly provided for in the statement of the law, all sorts of other factors (forces) may be present in the situation. If they are present, then the particle will not continue in its previous state of motion or rest (although that previous state will still have its nomic influence).

Newton's First Law is a conservation law, and many conservation laws are oaken laws. For instance, given an isolated system, energy is conserved. The energy of the system at a certain time determines that the system has that same energy at a latter time. But this law holds providing only that 'nothing interferes'.

148

But cannot an oaken law always be represented, in principle at least, as an iron law by putting in all the negative qualifications? Yes, in a way it can, provided that we bear in mind how wide the qualifications may be which are implied by the phrase 'in principle'. It could even be that the statement of, say, Newton's First Law as an iron law, would have to be of infinite length. This would be the case if the number of sorts of force capable of acting upon bodies was irreducibly infinite. But the vital point to remember is that the relation of necessitation present in each instantiation of the law involves only the actual universals involved. If negative universals are excluded as necessitating factors, then the absence of factors capable of interfering with the necessitation is *not* a factor in the necessitation.

It appears, then, that if N(F,G) is an oaken law, then all that is entailed is that *for all* x *where interfering conditions are absent, if* x *is F, then* x *is G*. The interfering conditions will be a perfectly determinate set of conditions, but it is logically possible that there are an infinite number of them. Note that the laws involving the interfering conditions may themselves be oaken.

Does this mean, then, that we need to recognize two sorts of necessitation, N_I and N_O, associated with iron and oaken laws respectively? I would hope to avoid this conclusion. I have up to this point written as if:

(1) N(F,G)

entails

(2) $(x) (Fx \supset Gx)$.

I now modify that claim. For there to be an entailment, the scope of (2) must be narrowed from *all Fs* to *all uninterfered with Fs*. An interfering property, I, is one such that if x is F and is I, then it is not a law that FIs are Gs. An uninterfered with instance of F is one which lacks any such further property I.

N(F,G) may now be said to be an iron law if and only if there does not, *as a matter of fact*, exist any such property I which is capable of interfering with Fs in this way. It will remain logically possible that there is such a property I, and so even in this case the strong *entailment* will not hold.

But might there not be laws which would, as it were, necessarily be iron laws, what one might dub 'steel' laws? Perhaps so. But such laws, I suggest, should be treated as second-order laws. It would be a law that all laws having certain property (perhaps a certain form) were laws where the corresponding universally quantified generalization held. It would be a *law* that all laws having property L exhibited the 'if N(F,G), then $(x) (Fx \supset Gx)$' pattern. This second-order law might in turn be iron or oaken, and, if iron, might be steel.

It is an important fact about a law whether it is iron or oaken. But, I suggest, the relation of necessitation, N, is the same in the two cases.

5 DISJUNCTIVE LAWS

Tooley has pointed out (1977, p. 677) that there might be laws having the form: it is a law that Fs are either Gs or Hs, but where there is no nomic factor differentiating the FGs and the FHs. The problem here is that *being G or H* is a disjunctive property and there are good reasons in the theory of universals to reject disjunctive properties. (See my 1978, Ch. 14.) How then should we analyse such a situation? Tooley takes the law to be a three-termed relation holding between the universals, F,G and H, with a construction-function taking these universals to the manifestation of the law: the quasi-uniformity that all Fs are either G or H. I, however, wish to treat the law as a species of necessitation instantiated in each of its instances. Can this be done in this sort of case without postulating disjunctive universals? A somewhat complex discussion proves necessary.

There are different possibilities here, which should first be sorted out. We are not interested in the case where it is a law that Fs are Gs, or a law that Fs are Hs, and still less in the case where both are laws. In all these cases the disjunction is trivially necessitated. (It could be treated as a derived law.) We are interested in the cases where there are Fs which are not Gs and are therefore Hs, and where there are Fs which are not Hs and are therefore Gs. Given the satisfaction of these two conditions, Gs and Hs might be related in three different ways. It might be logically impossible that Gs be Hs. It might be logically possible but physically impossible for Gs to be Hs. Finally, Gs which are Hs might be physically possible, and, let us assume, some Gs actually be Hs.

Let us begin with the simplest case, where G and H exclude each

150

other. We have the following nomic truths: Fs which are not Gs are Hs; and Fs which are not Hs are Gs. Considered separately, they appear to be each of them oaken laws. It is a law that Fs are Hs, except that this necessitation can be interfered with by the factor G. That is, if Fs are Gs, then the tendency of Fs to be Hs is interfered with by the addition of an extra factor. Again, it is a law that Fs are Gs, except that this necessitation can be interfered with by the factor H. That is, if Fs are Hs, then the tendency of Fs to be Gs is interfered with by the addition of an extra factor. Either law taken separately appears to present no difficulty, granted the distinction between iron and oaken laws.

Why, then, should it not be possible for both oaken laws to hold together? If so, the disjunctive law that an F must be a G or an H can be represented as a pair of oaken laws, laws which do not involve disjunctions.

This solution in terms of two oaken laws leaves an uneasiness which may be articulated thus. In order for Fs to be definitely Hs, or Gs, must they not first fail to be Gs, or fail to be Hs, and then, and only then, come to be Hs or come to be Gs? The failures would then be actual factors in the situation, which is what it is wished to deny.

However, if there is a worry here, then it seems to be a worry which is already involved in the original idea of a law which necessitates disjunctively. The law is such that if an F is not a G, then it must be an H, and if not an H, then it must be a G. So, for the F to be an H, say, must it not first have failed to be a G? Presumably this argument can be rejected, and, if it can be rejected, it can be rejected when the law is formulated as two oaken laws.

As David Lewis has pointed out to me, the worry may be particularly worrisome where what flows from being an F is something that occurs in the future. As Lewis says, two points are worth making in this connection. First, I regard the future as real. We are not to think of the present as the growing edge of being. Second, an *a* which is F at present, may become G after a certain interval of time, *t*. In that case, becoming G after interval *t* is a relational property of *a* now. It seems a perfectly good universal, and can therefore be a term in a relation of nomic necessitation. (See the next section.) Suppose, then, that we have an alleged irreducibly disjunctive law:

N(F, ((GvH) after interval *t*)).

My suggestion applied to this case is that this be broken up into two oaken laws:

(1) N(F, (G after interval t)) with (H after interval t) absent
(2) N(F, (H after interval t)) with (G after interval t) absent.

The sort of case which we have been considering is that where the properties G and H are logically incompatible, such as that where a quantum-mechanical system must pass into one of two incompatible energy-levels. What of the case where G and H are not logically incompatible, but nomically exclude each other? We want to deny, if at all possible, that here we have a case of an *underived* exclusion law.

This can be achieved without great difficulty. We already have the conditions that an F which is not a G must be an H, and an F which is not an H must be a G. We simply add that an F which is a G cannot be an H, and an F which is an H cannot be a G. The factors G and H exercise an inhibiting effect upon Fs, preventing them from being Hs and Gs respectively. Are these exclusion laws? They are, but we need not treat them as *underived* exclusion laws. Among the (positive) laws which govern Fs there are none which give Fs any probability of being (G&H)s. To produce this result is beyond an F's power. The exclusion law is supervenient upon the body of these positive laws.

We come finally to the case where some Fs are both Gs and Hs. For this case the two original oaken laws are required, and in addition a probabilistic law giving Fs a certain chance of acquiring the conjunctive property (G&H).

In this case we have three laws, the first two of them oaken:

(1) (N:1) (F,G), with H absent
(2) (N:1) (F,H), with G absent
(3) (N:P) (F, (G&H))

where P is less than 1. (The previous case was one where no such law as (3) holds.) These laws, however, will, taken just by themselves, permit the possibility of an F which is G by accident, and is H by accident. This, one might object, shows that the conjunction of (1) to (3) under-translates the statement 'it is a law that an F must be a G or an H'. For, in the double-accident case, the object's being F does not *determine* it to be anything, even disjunctively.

However, the double-accident case can be excluded by reformulating (1) as:

(1′) (N:1) (F,G) with the (N:1) (F,H) pattern absent.

(It will be remembered that laws are universals, and so are properties which can be absent from certain complex states of affairs.) This will ensure that if an F is H only by accident, then it is G by necessity. This will prevent a *double* accident. A parallel reformulation of (2) will ensure that, if the F is G only by accident, then it is H by necessity. Reformulation of both (1) and (2) will prevent any accident at all.

Besides ordinary disjunctive laws, Tooley also mentions the possibility of laws having the form that anything which lacks F has G (p. 677). As he remarks this can be rendered as a disjunctive law of universal scope: everything is either an F or a G. I, therefore, can render it as two oaken laws of universal scope. In the absence of property F, everything must be a G. In the absence of property G, everything must be an F. We can then use whatever is the correct account for laws of universal scope (see Sec. 2).

6 DO LAWS ALWAYS LINK THE PROPERTIES OF THE SAME OBJECT?

In the schematic laws which we have so far considered, it is a matter of one object having a property, and, as a result, having another property. It is this relation which has been symbolized by 'N'. But besides being deterministic, laws may be probabilistic, and the probabilities may take any of continuum-many values between 1 and 0. So N becomes a determinable whose determinates range from (N:1) down to (N: some infinitesimal > 0). Given the rejection of exclusion laws, (N:0) is rejected.

Restricting ourselves now for convenience to deterministic laws, can they all be given the form (N:1) (F,G)? We have seen the need to introduce higher-order laws, laws governing laws. Functional laws appear to be higher-order laws. Higher-order laws, however, exhibit the same form as first-order laws, but where the N relates higher-order universals. We have also seen the need to distinguish between underived and derived laws. Derived laws are mere deductions from the body of underived laws, and may take various forms, such as exclusion laws. It is, at best, *underived* deterministic laws which have a single form. Finally, we have distinguished between iron and oaken laws. With an iron law, (N:1) (F,G) holds, no matter what. It is a law that Fs are G. But with an oaken law there can be additional factors which, if present along with factor F, prevent Fs being Gs. (The absence of such factors is not a factor.) But, even if the law is oaken, it was argued that the relation which is instantiated in each instantiation is the same as that which would be instantiated if the law were an iron one, *viz.* (N:1) (F,G).

Exclusion laws we have rejected, or were at least inclined to reject, except as derived laws. If underived exclusion laws do have to be admitted, then it seems better to introduce negative universals rather than a new form of law. For in this way we can hold fast to the fruitful idea that laws are themselves universals instantiated in the instances of the law. If so, the law remains of the form (N:1) (F,G) with not-G as a substitution-instance for G. It may be remarked that if local laws have to be admitted, such as the case of Smith's garden, a quasi-universal, for instance *fruit in Smith's garden*, becomes a substitution-instance for one or more of the universals F and G.

Laws of universal scope may also apparently be reduced to the familiar form, one way or another. Tooley takes them to be higher-order laws to the effect that whatever property a thing has, it is a first-order law that something having that property has a further specified property. Forrest suggests that they are first-order laws, but involve a special antecedent universal, such as *being a first-order particular*.

In the previous section, it was argued that disjunctive laws: all Fs are either Gs or Hs: could be reduced to two oaken laws of orthodox form. A more desperate remedy would be to countenance the admission of disjunctive properties in such cases.

So far, then, it seems that we have been able to resist the suggestion that deterministic laws have any form except (N:1) (F,G).

But what now of cases where it is a law that, if something is F, then *something else* must be a G? A great deal can be done here by appealing to *relational properties*. Suppose it is a law that, if something is an F, then there exists something else, which is a G, and which stands to the F in the relation R, where F, G and R are genuine universals. We can reduce the law to the familiar form by saying that it is a law concerning Fs that they have the further relational property of *having R to a G*. This appears to be perfectly good consequent universal, which the universal F might necessitate. Once again we return to the form: it is a law that Fs are Gs.

It is to be noted, as already remarked in the previous section, that R may be, or may involve, a temporal relation. Indeed this will be the natural case. A set-up of the sort F may in time produce a G. The producing of a G, after a certain interval of time, would seem to be something which could be a relational property of Fs.

The question to be decided, however, is whether this appeal to relational properties is available in every case. Suppose it is a law that, if something is an F, then there exists something (the same thing or another thing) which is a G. It is not specified what relation the G must have to the F – simply that there must be such a G. Here, perhaps, we have a law not reducible to the standard form.

It is to be noted that even here there is dyadic predicate linking the F and the G. The F is *either the same as or distinct from* the G. But there is no reason to think that a genuine relation corresponds to this artificial predicate, and so the F will have no genuine relational property as a result.

The real question, however, is whether Fs and Gs could really be nomically linked in this utterly permissive way. Fs must be Gs, or something else must be G. Can the G be anywhere in space and time? Can it be in the past? If it cannot, we are beginning to set up *conditions* which the G must satisfy to be the G necessitated by this F. And then we are beginning to specify the *relationship* which the G must have to the F.

I leave the matter in suspense. It seems clear that, in the case of the law-statements with any empirical plausibility, it will be possible to find definite relations which the necessitated instance of G must have to the necessitating instance of F. It may be that there could be laws where this is not so.

But, with this dubious exception, I believe it may be plausibly claimed that laws can all be reduced to the F → G form. We need to specify the strength of the probability involved. But this may exhaust the possible forms of underived laws of nature.

7 FORMAL PROPERTIES OF NECESSITATION

What are the formal properties of the relation of necessitation? I shall argue that it is irreflexive, non-transitive, it does not contrapose, and, finally, that it is non-symmetrical. It is to be noticed that

155

the results hold as much for purely singular necessitation, if such a thing exists, as for relations between universals.

(1) First, the relation is necessarily irreflexive. a's being F cannot necessitate a's being F, nor can there be a law of nature of the form $N(F,F)$. This seems fairly obvious in itself. But in any case I believe that nothing is genuinely related to itself (Armstrong, 1978, Ch. 19, Sec. VI).

(2) It might seem that necessitation is necessarily transitive. If a's being F necessitates a's being G, and a's being G necessitates a's being H, must it not be that the case that a's being F necessitates a's being H? And if $N(F,G)$ and $N(G,H)$ obtain, then must it not be the case that $N(F,H)$? It is true that if $(N{:}.5)$ (F,G) and $(N{:}.5)$ $(F\&G,H)$, then it is false that $(N{:}.5)$ $(F,G\&H)$. But will it not be the case that $(N{:}.25)$ $(F,G\&H,)$? Will we not have a transmission of probabilities of which transitivity is a limiting case?

I do not think that this is correct. In the first place, any such transitivity will only hold subject to the condition that the laws involved are iron ones. But even if we presuppose this condition, transitivity fails to hold. What is then true is that if $N(F,G)$ and $N(G,H)$, then it is at least a *derived* law that Fs are Hs. But it need not be the case that $N(F,H)$. Similarly with probabilistic cases.

It is conceivable that $N(F,G)$, $N(G,H)$ and $N(F,H)$ should all obtain, three independent relations between universals. Suppose a to be F,G and H, and that all these laws hold. a's being H would then be a case of overdetermination. a would be H both because a was F and also because a was G. Special counterfactuals would hold. If the $F \rightarrow G$ law had not held, the $F \rightarrow H$ law would still have ensured that a was H. If the $F \rightarrow H$ law had not held, the combination of the $F \rightarrow G$ and $G \rightarrow H$ law would still have ensured that a was H.

(3) Contraposition fails to hold. If $N(F,G)$ then it is not the case that $N(\bar{G},\bar{F})$, because there are no such universals. However, provided that we have $N{:}1$, and also that $N(F,G)$ is an iron law, then it is a *derived* law that everything which is not a G is not an F. For cases of singular necessitation we have a derived counterfactual. If a's being F necessitates a's being G, then if a had not been G, a would not have been F.

(4) Finally, necessitation appears to be non-symmetrical. Clearly, it is not symmetrical. At one stage I was inclined to think it was asymmetrical. If $N(F,G)$, then it could not be the case that $N(G,F)$. The best that could obtain, I thought, was that it was a derived law

that Gs are Fs. I have been convinced that the conjunction of N(F,G) and N(G,F) is a logical possibility by considerations put to me by Tooley.

Consider the proposition that every state of affairs having the form F*a*, or some suitably selected sub-class of such states of affairs, has a prior cause. Such a proposition might be true. But not only that. Might it not be *a law of nature*? States of affairs, or states of affairs of a certain restricted sort, nomically must have prior causes. That is surely a possible law. If so, however, we will have to think of the state of affairs as necessitating the existence of the prior cause. (We will need to introduce appropriate universals.) The prior cause, however, also necessitates the state of affairs. Faced with this possibility, it seems that one must admit the possibility of symmetrical cases of necessitation.

It is true that this is not actually a case of N(F,G) and N(G,F). Instead, a general deterministic law would govern the necessity which runs from state of affairs to prior cause, and a particular causal law would govern the way the cause necessitated the state of affairs. Supposing the latter law to be N(F,G), there would be no necessity that N(G,F). Nevertheless, in the light of Tooley's argument, it is hard to see how we could deny that N(G,F) might hold.

Tooley's argument, incidentally, seems to show conclusively that there can be nomic necessitation which is not *causal* necessitation. If the existence of a suitable state of affairs necessitates a prior cause, this can hardly be a case of backward causation! So causal laws are a mere sub-species of the possible laws of nature.

What marks off the sub-species is not investigated in this work. (It is one of the topics taken up in a forthcoming work by Tooley.)

Returning now to the topic of this section, we can say that underived necessitation relations are necessarily irreflexive, not necessarily transitive, cannot be contraposed, and are non-symmetrical. It remains to argue that they are contingent rather than necessary.

11

Are the laws of nature necessary or contingent?

Suppose it to be granted that laws of nature, if underived, are irreducible relations between universals. Should those relations be thought of as holding necessarily? Must they obtain 'in every possible world'? Suppose that event a precedes event b by a certain interval of time. This is a first-order state of affairs having the form $R(a,b)$. It would be generally conceded that this state of affairs might have been other than it is. But suppose that we ascend to a second-order state of affairs, to a law of nature $N(F,G)$. Here, it may be argued, we have a state of affairs which could not be other than it is.

In what follows I shall argue, on the contrary, that $N(F,G)$ and $R(a,b)$ are both contingent states of affairs.

The obvious objection to the view that a true statement of a law of nature, such as '$N(F,G)$', is a necessary truth is that it is discovered to be true *a posteriori*, using the method of hypothesis, observation and experiment. By contrast, the necessary truths of logic and mathematics are, in general at least, established *a priori*, by thought, reason and calculation alone.

This argument is not conclusive. The distinction between truths known, or rationally believed, *a posteriori* and those known, or rationally believed, *a priori*, is an epistemological one. Kripke has raised the question why it should determine the *logical* status of the truths known, or rationally believed.

Nevertheless, in trying to discover the laws of nature, scientists feel free to consider possibilities in a very wide-ranging manner, quite unlike the constraints which naturally suggest themselves in logical and mathematical argument. It would have to be admitted, at the least, that the laws of nature give a definite impression of contingency. The onus of proof would therefore appear to be on those who maintain that the impression is mere illusion.

It may be, however, that this onus can be reversed. A traditional Rationalist line of thought here, put to me by Martin Tweedale, is to appeal to the Principle of Sufficient Reason. If a law such as N(F,G) is a mere contingent fact, then there is no sufficient reason why Fs should be Gs, rather than something else. But there ought to be such a reason.

To appeal to the Principle of Sufficient Reason is to insist that there must be an explanation why things are so rather than another way. The appeal must therefore enlist the sympathy of anybody who, like myself, looks to an account of laws which treats them as the explanations of regularities. Should we not go further and explain the laws themselves? To the extent that laws can be brought under higher-order laws, this can be done even by the Contingency view. But these higher-order laws will remain unexplained on that theory. There will be no sufficient reason for these laws.

The question arises, however, whether we cannot overdo that good thing: explanation. There is one philosophy which traces back all appearance of contingency to a single necessary being, the Absolute, which is the sole reality. That hypothesis, I believe, attempts to take explanation too far. A sign that this is so is that no serious and principled deduction of the phenomena from the One has ever been given, or looks likely to be given.

But if explanation has to stop short of the Absolute, then we have to accept brute fact, that is, contingency, at some point. At what point should we do this? That is a question of the utmost delicacy for every philosophy. In my judgement, the Regularity theory of law gives up much too soon. Instead, I have argued, regularities among particular states of affairs can be explained by connections between universals. Atomic connections of universals are substituted for molecular regularities. Can these connections in turn be explained? The system of connections may be simplified, and brought under higher-order laws. But when all this has been done, is there any hope of demonstrating the necessity of the ultimate connections? I do not believe that there is. Necessity can be asserted, but it cannot be demonstrated or even made plausible. That does not close the matter. But it does suggest that to appeal to Sufficient Reason here is to attempt to carry explanation too far.

An attempt which is sometimes made to back up this assertion is to argue that if the relation between the universals is contingent only, then it is possible that it should change over time, thus resurrecting at least the Problem of Induction. But to advance this argument is to demonstrate that one has lost one's grip upon what universals are. As already pointed out in Chapter 6, Section 1, it is not possible that both N(F,G) and ~N(F,G) should obtain. To add that one obtains at t, and the other at t_2, is confusion.

A second line of thought is to be found in Swoyer (1982). He argues that properties must have 'essential features'. He rejects the idea that these essential factors are phenomenal, or that they consist of properties of properties. By elimination, he reaches the idea that the essential features are the relations of 'nomic implication' which properties have to other properties

But why need properties have essential features at all? Perhaps their identity is primitive. To uphold this view is to reject the Principle of the Identity of Indiscernibles with respect to properties. Properties can just be different, in the same way that, many of us would maintain, ordinary particulars can just be different although having all their features in common. (For the latter, see my 1978, Ch. 9, Sec. I.) Swoyer objects to this view that the 'primitive' difference of ordinary particulars is grounded in something: their distinct spatio-temporal locations. But suppose, as seems thinkable, that there are particulars which are not spatio-temporal. *Pace* Aquinas, may not two angels simply be different from each other while having all the same properties? Apparently they would be primitively different. And why should not the same be true for properties? We might put the matter this way: properties can be their own essence.

It is to be noted, in any case, that if properties demand essential features, then it seems reasonable that these essential features should have essential features also. (If this further move is not necessary, why should the regress ever be embarked upon?) This will either lead to vicious infinite regress, or else to a *circle* of entities which provide essential features for each other. (I suppose that Swoyer thinks that the nomic network holding properties together creates such a circle.) But what of the circle as a whole? What is essential to it? Nothing, presumably. It is just itself. But if it can be just itself, why not a 'circle' of one, a single property which has no essential feature, but is instead just itself?

It may be noted, before leaving Swoyer, that he criticizes the view that laws of nature are contingent relations between universals by saying that it will involve 'cosmic coincidence' at the level of universals. This seems incorrect. The Regularity view does take a law to be a cosmic coincidence. But coincidence demands repetitions: this F is a G, that F is a G, and so on. If we have N(F,G) there is no *repetition*: it is, as Tooley puts it, an 'atomic fact'. All that is legitimate in Swoyer's complaint is that there is no *sufficient reason* for F bearing N to G.

I turn now to a much less global argument for the necessity of laws of nature, put forward by Sydney Shoemaker (1980). Shoemaker argues:

what makes a property the property it is, what determines its identity, is its potential for contributing to the causal powers of the things that have it. (p. 114)

From this he draws the conclusion, among others, that the link between a property and its potential effects is a necessary one. He says (p. 116) that his reason for holding this view is 'broadly speaking, epistemological'. Properties can only be known through their effects, ultimately their effects upon observers. If there were causally idle properties, then we could never have the slightest reason to believe in their existence. Again, if two different properties made exactly the same contribution to the causal powers of the things which had the properties, we would never have the slightest reason to believe that two properties were involved, rather than one. These epistemological points must be taken as clues to the ontology of the situation. Contribution to the causal powers of a thing determines the identity of properties.

In a note added in proof, Shoemaker accepts a criticism offered by Richard Boyd. Causal powers are powers to bring about certain sorts of effect. But the identity of a property is determined not simply by what it can help to bring about, but also by what can help to bring it about. Properties are what they are because they can contribute to bringing about certain effects, and because certain other properties can contribute to bringing it about that something possesses the property. It seems to me that at this point Shoemaker might as well adopt an explicitly *nomic* view of what determines a property to be what it is. A property is determined to be the particular property it is by the fact that it is nomically linked, in just certain ways, to just certain further properties. The necessity of the laws of nature will then be directly evident.

161

Epistemological arguments with ontological conclusions are notoriously difficult to estimate. I have already used at least one such argument myself in Chapter 9, Section 1. I there argued in the following way. Suppose that no Fs are Gs, omnitemporally. Suppose that there is no higher-order law from which a law giving a certain probability that an F is a G may be deduced counterfactually. We would then have no good reason to assert the existence of a law giving Fs a certain probability of being a G. I took this to be a clue to the ontology of the situation: in the circumstances, there can be no such law.

Notice, however, that my argument was not my sole, it was not even my main, argument for my conclusion. My main objection to admitting probabilistic laws in such a situation was that it would force us to admit at least the logical possibility of the ontological reality of uninstantiated laws and uninstantiated universals, a logical possibility which there is independent reason to reject. Shoemaker's case, however, seems to depend solely upon his epistemological argument. It is worth noticing here that from the *premiss* that the laws of nature are necessary, Shoemaker's rejection of idle properties, and rejection of different properties which make no nomic difference, cannot be extracted. For might there not be properties which of necessity are nomically idle? Might there not be two or more distinct properties from which identical nomic connections necessarily flowed? To rule out such possibilities, it seems that Shoemaker can only appeal to the fact that we could never have any good reason to assert that such possibilities are realized.

There is, however, one way in which Shoemaker might support his position further here. He could argue that a property is constituted by, is nothing but, its nomic links with other properties. Nomically idle properties would then be nothing, and properties with all the same nomic links would be the same property. This is a version of the view that properties are pure powers. The difficulty with this position is that it seems to lead either to infinite regress, or else to circularity, each of which appears to be vicious. If a property *is* nothing but its capacity to enter into nomic relations to further properties, the same must be said of these further properties, and so on indefinitely unless we return in a circle to the original property or properties. No property is anything in itself, but only in its relations to other properties as given by the laws of nature. But how can a system of things, each logically nothing in itself independently of

162

the system, be made into something by incorporation in the system? (See Swinburne, 1980, pp. 313–20, and Chapter 8, Section 3, of the present work.)

If an ontology of properties as pure powers is rejected, Shoemaker has only his epistemological argument to appeal to. But if one of the consequences of his argument, *viz.* the necessity of the laws of nature, turns out to have ontologically unacceptable consequences, that will be a good reason for rejecting his conclusion. In the rest of this chapter I hope to show that the Necessity theory is indeed ontologically unacceptable.

2 STRONG NECESSITY

Although I do not believe in the literal reality of possible worlds, or even in the literal reality of ways things might have been but are not, I know of no way to argue the question before us except by considering possible worlds. It may be that the necessary/contingent distinction is tied to a metaphysics which recognizes possibility as a real something wider than actuality. If this could be shown, then my inclination would be to abandon the necessary/contingent distinction and declare our present question about the status of the laws of nature unreal. But I cling to the hope that an account of 'possible worlds' can be given which does not assume the existence of *possibilia*. (My hope would be to give a *combinatorial* account of logical possibility, perhaps along the general lines of the *Tractatus*, but without a commitment to atomism. See Skyrms, 1981.) In the meanwhile, I discuss our question in terms of possible worlds.

Suppose, then, that the laws are necessary, and that it is a law that Fs are Gs. What does it mean to say that this law is necessary? One thing which might be meant is the assertion that:

$\square\,(N(F,G))$.

I will call this the doctrine of *Strong Necessity* with respect to laws. Our formula says that the universals F and G are related by the relation N in every possible world. That is, F,G and any other nomically related universals which there are, are *necessary beings*.

Martin Tweedale has objected to me (private correspondence) that there can be relations between non-existent items. For instance, of two specified grammars neither of which is the grammar of any actual language, one might be more powerful or more complex than

163

the other. As a result, although Tweedale agrees that universals are not necessary existents, and so do not exist in every possible world, still, he thinks, he can uphold the doctrine of the Strong Necessity of laws of nature.

To my mind it is very unsatisfactory to talk about relations between non-existents. It invites us into a Meinongian jungle, where I would not wish to go. It would be better, I think, to say that *if* there was a specified grammar G_1 and a specified grammar G_2, then G_1 would be more powerful than G_2. But, however we phrase the statement which compares the two grammars, the vital metaphysical point is that, like any other statement, it requires some truth-maker, and that truth-maker cannot be something non-existent. (In passing, I believe that this shows that we should accept that the past and the future exist.) What can that truth-maker be? In the case of the grammars, it is at least plausible that the truth-maker is the two *concepts* of the two grammars where concepts are actual mental entities. That G_1 is more powerful than G_2 is a *conceptual* truth. The necessity of $N(F,G)$, however, is presumably not a conceptual truth. What can *its* truth-maker be? Given that we work with possible worlds, which we have agreed to do, it seems that either F must exist in every possible world, and in each world have N to the universal G which also exists in that world, or else F must exist in some possible worlds only, and in those worlds have N to G. Tweedale has rejected the first alternative, and so must accept the second. This, however, as we shall see shortly, is the doctrine that the laws of nature are only *weakly* necessary, a view to be criticized in the next section.

I believe, then, that the Strong Necessity view of laws of nature does make the universals involved necessary beings. To my mind, to have drawn this consequence is already to have produced a good reason for denying that the laws of nature are strongly necessary.[1] For I maintain that universals are just as much contingent beings as particulars are.

---

[1] Although not relevant to the current argument, it is interesting to consider whether the principle: if the laws of nature are strictly necessary, then the related universals are necessary beings: can be converted. Given that universals are necessary beings, does it follow that their irreducible relations, and so the laws of nature, are necessary? One might invoke the principle: if the terms of a relation involve nothing but necessary beings, then the relation itself must hold necessarily. This principle has some plausibility. Apparently obvious counter-examples, such as co-instantiation by particulars, fail to respect the condition that the term of the relation involve

Worse follows, however. It is generally agreed that, whatever the status of universals, first-order particulars are contingent beings. If it is necessary that N(F,G), then F and G must exist in every universe, and be related by N. But there can be worlds where there are no Fs and no Gs. So, the doctrine of Strong Necessity is committed to uninstantiated universals. I maintain, however, that the Principle of Instantiation is a necessary truth. Universals, although real, are only abstractions from states of affairs, and so are incapable of existing in independence of states of affairs.[2] If universals could exist uninstantiated, then they would be substances, and would require a relation (a universal) to relate them to their particulars. The horrors of Bradley's regress would then be upon us (see Ch. 8, Sec. 2).

It is possible to treat those universals which figure in laws as necessary beings, that is, as existing in every possible universe, and yet still maintain the necessity of the Principle of Instantiation. But to do this it is further necessary to maintain that it is a necessary truth that every universal which can figure in a law is instantiated, at some time, in our universe (and every other). I do not know how to *show* that such a Principle of Plenitude is false or, if true, not necessarily true. But it does not seem a very plausible hypothesis! It seems logically possible that there might have been some other universals,

---

nothing but necessary beings. However, I do not know how to give positive arguments for the principle. I have argued in this work that laws of nature, that is, relations between universals, are themselves universals. If all universals are necessary beings, then the converted principle follows. But the doctrine of Strong Necessity does not demand that every universal be a necessary being. It only demands that universals which are nomically related be necessary beings. Grant that (N(F,G)) is a first-order universal. It is not automatically nomically related to anything. So it need not fall within the scope of the doctrine of Strong Necessity.

[2] Michael Tooley has suggested that it is possible to allow that universals can only exist in states of affairs, yet for these universals to be uninstantiated. Suppose that N(F,G) holds but there are no Fs or Gs. F and G are uninstantiated, but it can still be maintained that they exist only in a state of affairs: the second-order state of affairs, N(F,G). He suggests that we demand only of a universal that *either* it be 'saturated from the top' (figure in a higher-order state of affairs) *or* that it be 'saturated from the bottom' (have instances).

It seems to me, however, that the two forms of saturation differ markedly, and that 'saturation from the bottom' is always required. Notice that 'saturation from the top' has no theoretical upper limit, but that 'saturation from the bottom' ends with first-order particulars. Notice, further, that if (N(F,G)) is itself a universal, as I maintain, then if there are no Fs it will itself be unsaturated from the bottom, and *may* be unsaturated from the top, that is, not be a constituent of any higher-order state of affairs.

over and above the ones instantiated in our universe, obeying further laws.

I conclude then that, at the very least, a doctrine that the laws of nature are strongly necessary is incompatible with the view that universals are contingent beings.

3 WEAK NECESSITY

But this is not the end of the matter. As pointed out in particular by Swoyer (1982), it is still possible to defend what may be called a Weak Necessity theory.

Suppose it is held that Socrates is essentially human. This should not be rendered as:

☐ (Socrates is human).

Such a reading will have the human Socrates existing in every possible world, but, presumably, Socrates is a mere contingent being. What is wanted can be achieved by a weaker proposition:

☐ (Socrates exists ⊃ Socrates is human).

There will then be worlds in which Socrates exists, and worlds in which he does not. But in every world in which he does exist, he is human. (I hasten to add that I do not myself believe in essential properties, save relative to some conceptual scheme. The example was introduced only for purposes of illustration.)

Applying the same idea to an analysis of laws of nature as relations between universals, we render:

It is a law that Fs are Gs

as:

☐ (the universal F exists ⊃ N(F,G)).

This clever modification appears to enable one, should one so wish, to maintain the necessity of the laws of nature, yet evade the consequences just spelled out for the Strong Necessity theory. *In all and only those worlds which contain the universal F, it is a law that Fs are Gs.* It is then possible to maintain further that there are both worlds in which F exists *and worlds in which F does not exist*, that is, that F, like Socrates, is a contingent being. It can be further maintained, if we wish to maintain it, that it is a logically necessary condition for F to

166

exist in a world that F be at some place and time instantiated in that world, that F be 'saturated from below'. Or if, like Tooley, one rejects the necessity of the Principle of Instantiation, but still wishes, as he does, to maintain that universals are contingent beings, one can countenance worlds where F exists and is instantiated, worlds where F exists and is not instantiated and worlds where F does not exist at all. In every world of the first two sorts, and only in them, it is the case that N(F,G). In this way, the contingency of universals is combined with the necessity of laws.

In order now to investigate this suggestion, let us consider the case where it is a law that Fs which are Hs are Gs, but where Fs which are not Hs cannot be Gs. It seems clear that there are actual laws of this form. If so, they are possible. Now consider two sets of worlds: firstly, worlds which contain the universal F but not the universal H; second, worlds which contain both the universal F, the universal H and where some Fs are Hs.

In the latter set of worlds the law of nature N((F&H),G) obtains. The critical question is this: does this law hold in the first sort of world, where the universal H is lacking?

It seems that it cannot. For if the universal H is lacking, then at least one term is lacking in the relation between universals which constitutes the law. But if it does not, then can it really be said that the universal F is the same universal as the universal F in the worlds where the law does obtain? For to say that the laws of nature are necessary, even in the weak sense, is surely to say that the laws flow from the nature of the universals involved. The laws which they enter into are at least part of their being.

Should we then say that every world which contains the universal F must contain the universal H (and, perhaps, Fs which are Hs), and, indeed, every other universal to which F is nomically related? This is very counterintuitive. It is particularly unintuitive if we also wish to uphold the Principle of Instantiation for universals and for laws.

However, there is a natural compromise to be investigated. Considering the F-without-H worlds, may we not treat the N((F&H),G) law as a merely potential law in these worlds? *If* there were Hs (or uninstantiated H) in that sort of world, as there are not, then the law would obtain.

The critical question then arises what is the truth-maker, the ontological ground, for this counterfactual? Can it be simply this: in

167

all possible worlds where the universals F and H both exist (and, perhaps, are co-instantiated), it is a law that (F&H)s are Gs?

If this is a satisfactory answer, then it seems that the Weak Necessity view of the laws of nature can be upheld. But I do not find it satisfactory. For it seems, once again, that the necessary truth of the counterfactual must flow from the nature of the universal F, a nature which must be the same in every world, *including the worlds which lack H*. The truth-maker for the counterfactual must therefore be present in the H-lacking worlds. But there is no truth-maker available in such worlds.[3]

Or, rather, there is no truth-maker available in such worlds *unless we introduce irreducible powers* (as I think Shoemaker might). If the universal F necessarily bestows powers upon whatever particulars are F so that, if these particulars are also H, then those particulars further must be G, then it will not be necessary for the universal H also to exist. The universal F will be big with all its nomic potentialities, however impoverished the world in which it exists. These potentialities, which will include its potential to necessitate G *if* it, F, is co-instantiated with H, will serve as truth-maker for the law that $N((F\&H),G)$.

The old tradition which links powers with necessity is here upheld. The Weak Necessity view requires irreducible powers. But if we wish to uphold a purely Actualist metaphysics, then it seems that we should reject the Weak Necessity view of laws of nature and declare them to be contingent.

In the above argument, it was assumed that the universals which enter into laws are contingent beings. Suppose, however, that one also holds that these contingent beings must be instantiated to exist (an important motive for adopting the Weak Necessity theory). There is then a further embarrassment for the theory. In the case of a deterministic law, whether iron or oaken, the embarrassment does not arise. For instance, if $N(F,G)$ is a deterministic oaken law, then, in every world containing Fs which are not subject to one or more

---

[3] Dangerous as it is, perhaps it will help to see the force of this argument if I make an epistemological point. Suppose that our world contains F, but not H (or else contains H but no FHs). We want to know if it is a law that (F&H)→G. If the laws of nature are necessary, then must it not be possible in principle to discover that it is a law? But if the *only* truth-makers are states of affairs in merely possible worlds which contain both Fs and H, or those containing FHs, then, since we are not in those worlds, we would have no conceivable way of telling whether (F&H)→G holds or does not hold. So we want the law to flow from the nature of F.

of the possible interfering factors, it is an instantiated law that such Fs are Gs. Suppose, however, that the law is probabilistic only. To make the difficulty stand out clearly, let the probability be a very low one (but let the probabilistic law be iron). Let the law also not be derivable from some higher-order law.

The problem for the upholder of the Weak Necessity theory is now this. Should he or should he not allow worlds containing Fs which are not Gs? Suppose first that he allow such worlds. A Contingency theorist would simply allow such worlds on the grounds that, in them, the law fails to hold. But for the Weak Necessity theorist, where there are Fs, it is always a law that they have a certain chance of being Gs. So, if he allows worlds with Fs which are not G, then in these worlds the F→G law must hold but must be uninstantiated. If the law is a law not derived from some other laws he is then driven towards postulating an uninstantiated universal in that world (the universal G), contrary to hypothesis. (G might be instantiated elsewhere in the world, but there will be worlds in which it is not.)

The alternative for the upholder of the Weak Necessity theory is to say that in every world containing Fs the law is instantiated, however low the probability of instantiation is. This seems to be an arbitrary stipulation.

This difficulty may make us think that irreducibly probabilistic laws do not assort very well with a theory that laws are necessary.

4 UNINSTANTIATED LAWS

The necessity theory also has some problems with uninstantiated laws. We begin by recalling the distinction already made in Chapter 8, Section 5, between uninstantiated laws whose antecedents are nomically impossible, and those whose antecedents, though uninstantiated, are nomically possible. Mellor (1980, pp. 113–14) gives as an example of an uninstantiated law with nomically impossible antecedents the high temperature values of the vapour pressure law for water. That water decomposes below these temperatures is itself a law of nature. Newton's First Law, on the other hand, seems to be an uninstantiated law whose antecedent condition is nomically possible. A body not acted upon by a force would not be violating any law.

It seems, however, that the Necessity theory must give radically different accounts of these two sorts of laws. This is at least, a major inelegance of the theory.

Consider, first, uninstantiated laws with nomically *possible* antecedents. What is nomically possible is logically possible, and so the antecedent universal in the uninstantiated law is at least a logically possible existent. Now, either universals are necessary beings, or they are not. If they are necessary, they exist in the actual world, and so the antecedent universal in the uninstantiated law exists in the actual world and is suitably related to its consequent universal. This will be a completely Realistic account of such uninstantiated laws. If universals are contingent beings, then either it is logically possible for these contingent beings to exist uninstantiated, or it is not. If they can exist uninstantiated, then, presumably, uninstantiated laws in this world have as their antecedent universals such uninstantiated universals, which exist in this world. Again, we will have a completely Realistic account of uninstantiated laws (with nomically possible antecedents). Suppose, finally, that universals are contingent beings and it is logically impossible that they should exist uninstantiated. At least there will be other possible worlds in which the antecedent universals of the uninstantiated laws are instantiated. In each of these worlds the law will hold. This is at least a quasi-Realistic account of these sorts of uninstantiated law.

But now consider uninstantiated laws of nature with nomically impossible antecedents. As Mellor points out, if the laws of nature are necessary (it seems to be irrelevant whether the necessity is Strong or Weak), then such laws will have *logically* impossible antecedents. Such laws, then, correspond to nothing at all in any world. The best which could be claimed for them is that they are vacuously true. Then, however, there would follow the unacceptable conclusion that a 'law' with the same impossible antecedent and a consequent logically incompatible with the original consequent would also be true.

Mellor takes the argument of the previous paragraph to be enough to refute the notion that the laws of nature are necessary. This seems to me to be too optimistic. The Necessity theorist may be able to give some account of the truth-conditions of statements of uninstantiated law with nomically impossible antecedents. Consider a parallel. In order to prove a theorem, P, a mathematician may begin by assuming that ~P. From this premiss he may deduce Q, which involves a contradiction, and so prove P. Now consider his statement 'if ~ P, then Q'. Here a hypothetical connection is asserted, but one, presumably, with a logically impossible antecedent. Yet, if he is a good mathematician, it may be in some sense *true*, a sense in which 'if ~P, then ~Q' is not true. Difficult it may be to give truth-conditions for this statement 'if ~P, then Q', but we do not doubt that it has truth-conditions.

The upholder of the Necessity theory of laws may therefore maintain that there can be 'true' statements of uninstantiated law with nomically impossible conditions. Their truth-conditions will perhaps resemble the conditions for the mathematician's 'if ~P, then Q'.

But Mellor's argument has its force, even if he has overestimated that force. An upholder of the Necessity theory of laws must drive a deep wedge between uninstantiated laws with nomically possible antecedents and uninstantiated laws with impossible antecedents. Whatever account he gives of the latter it cannot be the same account which he gives of the former. But, as Mellor says, this seems very arbitrary. Scientists make no such sharp distinction between the two sorts of uninstantiated law.

The argument is far from conclusive. But it is an unhappy consequence of the Necessity theory.

Conclusions

I will try to sum up the main positive theses argued for in this essay.

Laws of nature are dyadic relations of necessitation (or probabili-
fication) holding between universals. They are (higher-order) states
of affairs, states of affairs which are simultaneously universals. The
instantiations of these universals are the positive instances falling
under the law. It is an intelligible notion that a particular first-order
state of affairs should necessitate a further first-order state of affairs,
yet not in virtue of the universals involved in these states of affairs.
But in a law of nature this *same* relation of necessitation links *sorts* of
states of affairs, that is, universals. Such necessitations 'might have
been other than they are', that is, they are contingent. Where one
sort of state of affairs necessitates another, then it is entailed, in the
absence of further interfering factors (which are always at least logically possible), that the first sort of state of affairs is constantly
conjoined with the second sort of state of affairs.

All genuine laws are instantiated laws. Statements of uninstantiated law are to be construed as counterfactuals about what laws
would hold if certain conditions were realized. Such statements
depend for their truth upon the existence of higher-order laws.
Given the higher-order law and the contrary-to-fact condition, then
the uninstantiated law may be deduced.

Functional laws are higher-order laws governing those lower-
order laws which can be deduced from a functional law after
substituting particular values for independent variables. Higher-
order laws are relations between higher-order universals. These
higher-order universals are instantiated by the lower-order universals involved in the lower-order laws. (*Mass* may be a higher-order
universal, instantiated by the determinate mass-values such as one
kilogram exact.)

Irreducibly probabilistic laws are also relations between universals. These relations give (are constituted by) a certain objective
probability that individual instantiations of the antecedent universal

172

will *necessitate* instantiation of the consequent universal. They give a probability of a necessitation in the particular case. Like all laws, they must have (positive) instantiations at some time. Deterministic laws are limiting cases of probabilistic laws (probability 1).

It is always logically possible that the antecedent universal of a law of nature should be instantiated, yet that, because of the presence of interfering factors, the consequent universal not be instantiated. (The absence of interfering factors is not a factor.) If this possibility is no more than a logical possibility, then the law may be said to be iron. (A probabilistic law can be an iron law.) If interference sometimes actually occurs, then the law may be said to be oaken.

There are strong, if not conclusive, reasons to reject negative and disjunctive universals. As a result, there is reason to reject exclusion laws, and laws with disjunctive consequents. However, such laws may be freely admitted as *derived* laws. Derived laws are no more than the logical consequences of the underived or genuine laws. They involve no further universals or relations between universals.

It appears that all laws link a state of affairs where a particular has a property with a state of affairs where *that same particular* has a further property. However, the properties involved may be *relational* properties. The relations involved in these relational properties will regularly involve temporal relations.

The necessitation relation, unlike logical necessitation, is not reflexive, is not transitive, cannot be contraposed, and is not symmetrical.

Works cited

Anscombe, G.E.M. (1971) *Causality and Determination*, Cambridge University Press, reprinted in *Causation and Conditionals*, ed. E. Sosa, Oxford University Press, 1975

Armstrong, D.M. (1973) *Belief, Truth and Knowledge*, Cambridge University Press

Armstrong, D.M. (1978) *Universals and Scientific Realism*, 2 vols., Cambridge University Press

Ayer, A.J. (1956) What is a Law of Nature? *Revue Internationale de Philosophie*, 10, reprinted in Ayer, *The Concept of a Person*, London: Macmillan, 1963

Beauchamp, T.L. (1972) Cosmic Epochs and the Scope of Scientific Laws, *Process Studies*, 2

Berkeley, G. *Essay towards a New Theory of Vision, Works*, ed. A.A. Luce and T.E. Jessop, Vol 1, London: Nelson, 1948

Bradley, M. (1979) Critical Notice of D.M. Armstrong's *Universals and Scientific Realism, Australasian Journal of Philosophy*, 57

Braithwaite, R.B. (1927) The Idea of Necessary Connection, *Mind*, 36

Braithwaite, R.B. (1968) *Scientific Explanation*, Cambridge University Press

Broad, C.D. (1935) Mechanical and Teleological Causation, *Proceedings of the Aristotelian Society*, Supp. Vol. 14, reprinted in *Induction, Probability and Causation*, Selected Papers by C.D. Broad, Dordrecht: Reidel, 1968

Davidson, D. (1967) Causal Relations, *Journal of Philosophy*, 64, reprinted in *Causation and Conditionals*, ed. E. Sosa, Oxford University Press, 1975

Dretske, F.I. (1977) Laws of Nature, *Philosophy of Science*, 44

Fodor, J.A. (1974) Special Sciences (or: The Disunity of Science as a Working Hypothesis), *Synthese*, 28

Foster, J. (1979) In *Self*-defence, in *Perception and Identity*, ed. G.F. Macdonald, London: Macmillan

Goodman, N. (1954) *Fact, Fiction and Forecast*, Atlantic Highlands, N.J.: The Athlone Press

Hempel, C.G.(1945) Studies in the Logic of Confirmation, reprinted in Hempel, *Aspects of Scientific Explanation*, New York: The Free Press, 1965

Hume, D. *A Treatise of Human Nature*, 2 vols., Everyman, 1911

Hume, D. *Inquiry concerning Human Understanding*, ed. L.A. Selby-Bigge,

Oxford University Press, 1946

Johnson, W.E. (1924) *Logic, Part III*, Cambridge University Press

Kneale, W.C. (1950) Natural Laws and Contrary-to-fact Conditionals, *Analysis*, 10, reprinted in *Philosophical Problems of Causation*, ed. T.L. Beauchamp, Belmont, Cal.: Dickenson, 1974

Kneale, W.C. (1961) Universality and Necessity, *British Journal for the Philosophy of Science*, 12, reprinted in *Philosophical Problems of Causation*, ed. T.L. Beauchamp, Belmont, Cal.: Dickenson, 1974.

Lewis, D.K. (1973) *Counterfactuals*, Oxford: Basil Blackwell

Mackie, J.L. (1966) Counterfactuals and Causal Laws, in *Analytical Philosophy: First Series*, ed. R.J. Butler, Oxford: Basil Blackwell

Mackie, J.L. (1974) *The Cement of the Universe*, Oxford University Press

Mackie, J. L. (1979) A Defence of Induction, in *Perception and Identity*, ed. G.F. Macdonald, London: Macmillan

Mellor, D.H. (1974) In Defence of Dispositions, *Philosophical Review*, 83

Mellor, D.H. (1980) Necessities and Universals in Natural Laws, in *Science, Belief and Behaviour*, ed. D.H. Mellor, Cambridge University Press

Molnar, G. (1969) Kneale's Argument Revisited, *Philosophical Review*, reprinted in *Philosophical Problems of Causation*, ed. T.L. Beauchamp, Belmont, Cal.: Dickenson, 1974

Moore, G.E. (1925) A Defence of Common Sense, in *Contemporary British Philosophy (Second Series)* ed. J.H. Muirhead, London: Macmillan

Musgrave, A. (1981) Wittgensteinian Instrumentalism, *Theoria*, 47

Pap, A. (1962) *An Introduction to the Philosophy of Science*, Free Press of Glencoe

Plato, *Phaedo*, trans. D. Gallop, Oxford University Press, 1975

Popper, K.R. (1959) *The Logic of Scientific Discovery*, London: Hutchinson

Ramsey, F.P. (1929) General Propositions and Causality, reprinted in Ramsey (1978)

Ramsey, F.P. (1978) *Foundations*, ed. D.H. Mellor, London: Routledge & Kegan Paul

Shoemaker, S. (1980) Causality and Properties, in *Time and Cause*, ed. P. Van Inwagen, Dordrecht: Reidel

Skyrms, B. (1980) *Causal Necessity*, New Haven, Conn.: Yale University Press

Skyrms, B. (1981) Tractarian Nominalism, *Philosophical Studies*, 40

Stove, D.C. (1973) *Probability and Hume's Inductive Scepticism*, Oxford University Press

Strawson, P.F. (1952) *An Introduction to Logical Theory*, London: Methuen

Suchting, W.A. (1974) Regularity and Law, in *Boston Studies in the Philosophy of Science*, ed. R.S. Cohen, and M.W. Wartofsky, Dordrecht: Reidel

Swinburne, R. (1980) Properties, Causation and Projectibility: Reply to Shoemaker, in *Applications of Inductive Logic*, ed. L.J. Cohen, and M. Hesse, Oxford University Press

Swoyer, C. (1982) The Nature of Natural Laws, *Australasian Journal of Philosophy*, 60

175

Tooley, M. (1977) The Nature of Laws, *Canadian Journal of Philosophy*, 7
Van Fraassen, B.C. (1980) *The Scientific Image*, Oxford University Press
Whitehead, A.N. (1933) *Adventures of Ideas*, Harmondsworth, Middx: Penguin Books
Williams, D.C. (1947) *The Ground of Induction*, Cambridge, Mass.: Harvard University Press
Wittgenstein, L. (1921) *Tractatus Logico-Philosophicus*, translated by D.F. Pears and B.F. McGuiness, London: Routledge & Kegan Paul 1961

Index

177